The Challenging Conversation

Skills and Strategies for Dealing with Difficult People

Rachel Kim

Table of Contents

INTRODUCTION

In our journey through life, we all encounter difficult people—individuals who seem determined to test our patience, challenge our composure, and leave us feeling drained and frustrated. Whether it's the irate customer, the passive-aggressive colleague, the argumentative family member, or the unreasonable boss, these challenging interactions are an inevitable part of the human experience.

But what if I told you that these encounters, as vexing as they may be, hold within them the potential for growth, understanding, and resolution? This book, "The Challenging Conversation: Skills and Strategies for Dealing with Difficult People," is your guide to transforming these seemingly insurmountable obstacles into opportunities for constructive communication and personal empowerment.

In these pages, we will explore the intricacies of human behavior, delve into the psychology behind difficult personalities, and equip you with the tools and techniques needed to navigate these challenging conversations with confidence and grace. From understanding the root causes of difficult behavior to mastering the art of active listening, from setting boundaries effectively to resolving conflicts at work and in personal relationships—this book offers a comprehensive roadmap to enhance your communication skills and build more harmonious connections.

The ability to participate in challenging conversations is not just a valuable skill; it is an essential life skill. It empowers you to transform conflict into cooperation, frustration into empathy, and discord into collaboration. So, if you're ready to embark on a journey of personal growth and improved relationships, turn the page and let's begin the transformational journey of mastering "The Challenging Conversation."

CHAPTER I

Understanding Difficult People

Types of difficult personalities

Dealing with difficult people is an inevitable part of life, whether in our personal relationships, professional settings, or even chance encounters in public spaces. Understanding the types of difficult personalities we may encounter is essential for effective communication and conflict resolution. These personalities manifest in various ways, each presenting its unique set of challenges. In this section, we will explore some common types of difficult personalities, shedding light on their characteristics and behaviors.

One of the most recognizable types of difficult personalities is the "Aggressive" individual. These people are often assertive to the point of being confrontational. They tend to raise their voice, use offensive language, and resort to intimidation tactics to get their point across. Aggressive personalities can be exhausting to deal with, as their approach can make conversations feel like battlegrounds. However, it's essential to recognize that their aggression is often a defense mechanism, masking insecurities or deep-seated frustrations. Managing aggressive personalities requires remaining calm, setting boundaries, and redirecting the conversation toward a more constructive path.

On the opposite end of the spectrum, we have "Passive" individuals. These individuals avoid confrontation at all costs, often to their detriment. Passive personalities have difficulty expressing their needs, opinions, or feelings.

They tend to say yes when they mean no, suppress their emotions, and allow others to dictate the terms of a conversation or relationship. While passive individuals may seem easy to get along with, their inability to communicate effectively can lead to misunderstandings and unmet expectations. Dealing with passive personalities involves encouraging open dialogue, actively seeking their input, and providing a safe space for them to express themselves.

"Passive-Aggressive" personalities combine aspects of both aggression and passivity. These individuals may appear agreeable on the surface but harbor resentment or anger beneath. Instead of addressing issues directly, they resort to subtle, often underhanded, behaviors to express their frustration. This might include sarcasm, backhanded compliments, or procrastination. Passive-aggressive behavior can be perplexing, as it leaves the other party unsure about the true intentions or grievances of the person. Effectively handling passive-aggressive individuals necessitates addressing issues head-on, encouraging open communication, and seeking clarity on their concerns.

Some individuals exhibit "Narcissistic" traits, which can make conversations challenging due to their excessive self-centeredness and lack of empathy. Narcissistic personalities believe they are exceptional and entitled to special treatment. They often dismiss the feelings and perspectives of others, manipulate conversations to revolve around themselves, and are quick to criticize or belittle those who challenge their views. Dealing with narcissistic personalities requires setting clear boundaries, maintaining assertiveness, and recognizing that their behavior is a reflection of their insecurities rather than a judgment of your worth.

"Manipulative" personalities are adept at controlling situations and people to their advantage. They often use charm, flattery, or guilt-tripping to achieve their goals. Manipulative individuals may downplay their own responsibilities while subtly coercing others into fulfilling their needs or desires. Their tactics can be insidious, leaving those around them feeling manipulated or used. To counter manipulative behavior, it's essential to stay vigilant, set boundaries, and avoid being drawn into their web of deceit.

In contrast, "Critical" personalities are quick to find fault in others and are often overly judgmental. They nitpick, criticize, and seldom offer praise or support. Interactions with critical individuals can lead to feelings of inadequacy and self-doubt. To navigate conversations with critical personalities, it's crucial to remain confident in your abilities, acknowledge their critiques when valid, and diplomatically address unfounded criticism.

"Needy" personalities require constant validation and attention. They may be overly reliant on others for emotional support or approval. While it's natural for individuals to seek connection, needy personalities can be draining, as they often demand an excessive amount of time and energy. Dealing with needy personalities involves setting clear boundaries, encouraging self-sufficiency, and offering support without enabling dependency.

Finally, "Dramatic" personalities tend to exaggerate situations and emotions, making every issue seem like a crisis. They thrive on attention and may create unnecessary turmoil. Conversations with dramatic individuals can be exhausting, as they often steer discussions toward emotional extremes. To manage interactions with dramatic personalities, it's essential to remain calm, seek clarity, and avoid getting caught up in unnecessary drama.

In conclusion, recognizing and understanding the various types of difficult personalities is a crucial step in effective communication and conflict resolution. Each type of difficult personality presents its unique set of challenges, but with patience, empathy, and appropriate strategies, it is possible to navigate conversations and relationships with these individuals more successfully. By gaining insight into their behavior and motivations, we can foster healthier interactions and, in some cases, even help these individuals address their own underlying issues. Ultimately, improving our skills in dealing with difficult personalities can lead to more harmonious and productive relationships in both our personal and professional lives.

Psychological insights into difficult behavior

Human behavior is an intricate interplay of emotions, thoughts, and experiences. When we encounter difficult behavior in others, it can be perplexing and frustrating. However, delving into the psychological aspects of difficult behavior can provide valuable insights into why people act the way they do. In this section, we will explore the psychological underpinnings of difficult behavior, shedding light on the factors that contribute to challenging interpersonal interactions.

One of the key psychological insights into difficult behavior is the concept of defense mechanisms. Defense mechanisms are unconscious psychological processes that individuals employ to protect themselves from uncomfortable emotions or thoughts. When people face situations that trigger anxiety, shame, or guilt, they often resort to defense mechanisms as a way of coping. For example, an individual may employ the defense mechanism of "projection" by attributing their own undesirable qualities or emotions to others. This can manifest as blame or criticism, making it difficult to engage in productive conversations. Understanding defense mechanisms can help us recognize when someone is using them and empathize with their underlying emotional struggles.

Another psychological insight into difficult behavior is the impact of past experiences and traumas. Often, individuals who exhibit challenging behavior have a history of adverse events or unresolved traumas that influence their current actions and reactions. These past experiences can shape their worldviews, affecting how they perceive and respond to different situations. For example, someone who has experienced betrayal in the past may struggle with trust issues, leading to skepticism and defensiveness in their interactions. Recognizing the role of past experiences in difficult behavior can foster empathy and patience in dealing with such individuals.

Moreover, challenging behavior is significantly shaped by cognitive biases. Our brains use mental shortcuts, or cognitive biases, to process information more quickly. These short cuts, though, may result in skewed perceptions and conclusions. One prevalent cognitive bias is "confirmation bias," in which people ignore or minimize contradicting evidence in favor of seeking out and interpreting data that supports their preexisting beliefs. This can lead to stubbornness and resistance to alternative viewpoints, making it challenging to engage in rational discussions. Recognizing cognitive biases, both in ourselves and others, is essential for promoting open-mindedness and constructive dialogue.

Emotional intelligence is another psychological insight that can help us understand and address difficult behavior. Emotional intelligence is the ability to determine, understand, as well as manage one's own emotions, as well as the emotions of others. Individuals with lower emotional intelligence may struggle to regulate their emotions, leading to outbursts, mood swings, or irrational behavior during challenging situations. They may also struggle to empathize with the emotions of others, which can hinder effective communication. By fostering emotional intelligence, individuals can learn to navigate their emotions and respond to difficult situations with greater self-awareness and empathy.

Personality traits is also significant in shaping difficult behavior. The field of psychology has identified various personality traits that can contribute to challenging interpersonal interactions. For instance, individuals with high levels of narcissism tend to exhibit entitlement, lack of empathy, and a constant need for admiration. This can result in self-centered and manipulative behavior, making it difficult to establish healthy relationships. Similarly, individuals with high levels of perfectionism may set unrealistic standards for themselves and others, leading to critical and demanding behavior. Recognizing these personality traits can help us tailor our approach when dealing with difficult individuals, emphasizing empathy and assertiveness as needed.

In some cases, mental health issues are at the root of difficult behavior. Conditions such as anxiety disorders, depression, borderline personality disorder, or substance abuse disorders can significantly impact an individual's behavior and interpersonal relationships. For instance, someone with social anxiety may come across as distant or avoidant in social situations, while a person with borderline personality disorder may struggle with intense mood swings and difficulty maintaining stable relationships. Understanding the influence of mental health on behavior is crucial for approaching these individuals with compassion and encouraging them to seek appropriate support and treatment.

Furthermore, situational factors can also contribute to difficult behavior. External stressors, like financial difficulties, work pressures, or family conflicts, can trigger emotional responses that spill over into interactions with others. People may use defense mechanisms, like displacement or projection, to cope with their stress, leading to conflicts with those around them. Recognizing the impact of situational factors on behavior allows us to approach challenging situations with empathy and offer support to those who may be struggling.

In conclusion, gaining psychological insights into difficult behavior is essential for fostering understanding and empathy in our interactions with others. Recognizing the role of defense mechanisms, past experiences, cognitive biases, emotional intelligence, personality traits, mental health issues, and situational factors can help us navigate challenging interpersonal interactions more effectively. Instead of viewing difficult behavior as merely problematic, we can approach it with a deeper understanding of the underlying psychological dynamics at play. This can lead to more productive conversations, improved relationships, and the potential for personal growth and healing, both for ourselves and those exhibiting difficult behavior.

The impact of difficult people on personal and professional life

Difficult people are a ubiquitous presence in our personal and professional lives. Whether they're found in our families, social circles, or workplaces, their impact can be profound and far-reaching. This section explores the various ways in which difficult individuals can affect our personal and professional spheres, shedding light on the challenges they pose and strategies for mitigating their negative influence.

In the realm of personal life, the presence of difficult people can lead to significant emotional stress and strain on relationships. For instance, dealing with a difficult family member, such as a narcissistic parent or a passive-aggressive sibling, can take a toll on one's mental and emotional well-being. These individuals often bring conflict, manipulation, and emotional turmoil into family dynamics, making it challenging to maintain healthy and loving relationships. Constant exposure to such behavior may lead to anxiety, depression, and a sense of powerlessness within the family unit.

Moreover, difficult people can negatively impact our friendships and social circles. A toxic friend who exhibits traits like jealousy, manipulation, or constant negativity can drain our energy and erode our self-esteem over time. Such relationships can lead to isolation as individuals seek to distance themselves from the emotional toll inflicted by these friends. The stress of managing these social dynamics can result in decreased overall life satisfaction and happiness.

In the professional realm, the presence of difficult colleagues or superiors can hinder career growth and job satisfaction. An aggressive coworker who frequently engages in confrontations or a micromanaging boss who stifles autonomy can create a hostile work environment. This can lead to decreased productivity, increased job stress, and a toxic workplace culture that impacts not only the targeted individual but also the entire team. In extreme cases, it can result in burnout, turnover, and a loss of talent for the organization.
Difficult people can also hinder professional networking and collaboration. Their abrasive behavior, poor communication skills, or inability to work well with others can make it challenging to establish valuable connections within one's industry. Opportunities for collaboration and career advancement may be missed due to the strained relationships created by these individuals.

Furthermore, the impact of difficult people on personal and professional life extends beyond immediate emotional and relational challenges. Such interactions can have long-lasting effects on mental health and well-being.

Chronic exposure to stress, conflict, and negativity can contribute to anxiety disorders, depression, and other mental health issues. In turn, these mental health challenges can spill over into other areas of life, affecting personal relationships and job performance.

In personal life, the constant presence of difficult people may lead to a sense of hopelessness and resignation. Individuals may find themselves questioning their self-worth or doubting their ability to maintain healthy relationships. This can result in social withdrawal and isolation as individuals seek to protect themselves from further emotional harm.

In the professional arena, the impact of difficult colleagues or superiors can undermine confidence and career progression. Constant criticism, belittling, or bullying can erode an individual's self-esteem, making it difficult for them to assert themselves and pursue advancement opportunities. Additionally, the stress and anxiety associated with difficult work environments can result in physical health issues, such as insomnia, headaches, and digestive problems, further complicating an individual's overall well-being.

Despite the considerable challenges posed by difficult people, there are strategies as well as coping mechanisms that can help mitigate their impact. In personal life, setting boundaries is crucial. Establishing clear limits on what behavior is acceptable and communicating these boundaries assertively can help protect one's emotional well-being. Seeking support from friends, family, or therapists can also provide a valuable outlet for processing emotions and gaining perspective on difficult relationships.

In the professional realm, addressing issues with difficult colleagues or superiors through appropriate channels, such as HR departments or supervisors, can be an effective way to mitigate their impact. Documenting instances of problematic behavior can provide evidence if further action is necessary. Additionally, building a strong support network within the workplace, including relationships with colleagues who share similar experiences, can offer emotional support and guidance.

Another valuable strategy for dealing with difficult people in both personal and professional life is developing effective communication skills. Learning how to assert oneself, express needs and boundaries, and engage in constructive conflict resolution can empower individuals to navigate challenging interactions more effectively. It can also help to diffuse tension and promote healthier relationships.

Furthermore, practicing emotional intelligence can be a powerful tool for managing the impact of difficult people. Developing the ability to recognize and regulate one's own emotions, as well as empathize with the emotions of others, can lead to a more efficient communication and conflict resolution. It can also help individuals maintain their composure in the face of challenging behavior.

In conclusion, the presence of difficult people in personal and professional life is an unavoidable aspect of human interaction. These individuals can have a deep impact on our emotional well-being, relationships, and career satisfaction. However, by recognizing the challenges they pose and employing strategies such as setting boundaries, effective communication, and emotional intelligence, we can mitigate their negative influence. Ultimately, the ability to navigate interactions with difficult people is a valuable skill that can lead to greater resilience, healthier relationships, and increased overall well-being in both personal and professional domains.

CHAPTER II

Preparation for Challenging Conversations

Self-assessment: Are you part of the problem?

In the realm of personal and professional relationships, it's easy to perceive difficult people as the primary source of conflict and tension. We often find ourselves pointing fingers and attributing the difficulties we face to their behavior, personality traits, or communication style. However, it's essential to take a step back and engage in a process of self-assessment. Are we, in any way, contributing to the problem? In this section, we will explore the concept of self-assessment and its significance in dealing with difficult people.

Self-assessment involves an honest and critical examination of our thoughts, actions, and behaviors in interpersonal interactions. It's an opportunity to take a closer look at our role in conflicts and challenges. When dealing with difficult people, the inclination to blame them entirely can be a barrier to resolution and personal growth. By turning the spotlight inward and assessing our own behavior, we gain valuable insights into how we may inadvertently exacerbate difficult situations.

One critical aspect of self-assessment is examining our own triggers and emotional responses. Difficult people often have a knack for pushing our buttons, evoking strong emotional reactions. These reactions can cloud our judgment and escalate conflicts. It's essential to ask ourselves why certain behaviors or comments trigger such strong emotions. Are there unresolved past experiences or personal insecurities that contribute to our reactions? Recognizing our triggers can help us respond more rationally and constructively in challenging situations.

Another aspect of self-assessment involves examining our communication style. Effective communication is a two-way street, and our own communication patterns can either facilitate or hinder conflict resolution. Do we tend to be passive-aggressive or overly confrontational? Do we struggle with active listening and empathy? Are we open to feedback and willing to compromise? Assessing our communication habits allows us to identify areas for improvement and adjust our approach when interacting with difficult people.

Furthermore, self-assessment involves reflecting on our own expectations and boundaries. Unrealistic expectations or a failure to set clear boundaries can contribute to conflicts with difficult individuals. Are we expecting too much from others? Are our boundaries too rigid or too lax? It's essential to evaluate whether our expectations align with reality and whether our boundaries are healthy and conducive to productive relationships.

Self-awareness is a key component of self-assessment. It demands introspection and a willingness to confront our own shortcomings. Self-awareness allows us to recognize patterns of behavior that may be contributing to conflicts with difficult people. It also empowers us to take responsibility for our actions and make positive changes in our interactions.

Taking responsibility for our role in conflicts with difficult people can be a challenging endeavor. It requires humility and a willingness to acknowledge our own imperfections. However, this self-awareness is a powerful catalyst for personal growth and improved relationships. When we recognize that we are part of the problem, we gain agency and the ability to make constructive changes.

Self-assessment also involves seeking feedback from trusted individuals. Sometimes, we may not be fully aware of the impact of our behavior on others. Seeking honest feedback from friends, family, or colleagues can provide valuable insights into how our actions may contribute to conflicts. It's essential to approach this feedback with an open mind and a willingness to learn.

One of the most significant benefits of self-assessment is its potential to de-escalate conflicts with difficult people. When we take ownership of our role in a conflict and approach the situation with a willingness to change, it can diffuse tension and create an atmosphere of cooperation. Difficult individuals may also be more receptive to resolving conflicts when they see that we are taking their concerns seriously and making efforts to improve the relationship.

Self-assessment is not a one-time endeavor but an ongoing process. It requires continuous reflection and self-improvement. As we become more self-aware and better at recognizing our own contributions to conflicts, we can develop healthier communication habits, set more realistic expectations, and establish firmer boundaries. This, in turn, can lead to more harmonious relationships with difficult people.

In conclusion, self-assessment is a valuable tool in dealing with difficult people. It involves examining our own triggers, communication style, expectations, and boundaries. It requires self-awareness and a willingness to take responsibility for our role in conflicts. By engaging in self-assessment, we can de-escalate conflicts, foster personal growth, and improve our relationships with difficult individuals. Ultimately, it empowers us to be more effective communicators and more adaptable in navigating the complexities of human interactions. So, the next time you find yourself in conflict with a difficult person, take a moment to ask, "Am I part of the problem?" It may lead to transformative insights and more constructive resolutions.

Setting clear goals and objectives

Challenging conversations are an inevitable part of our personal and professional lives. Whether it's addressing conflicts with colleagues, navigating sensitive issues with loved ones, or dealing with difficult individuals, these interactions can be emotionally taxing and potentially unproductive. However, one effective strategy for navigating challenging conversations is to set clear goals and objectives. In this section, we will explore how the practice of setting clear goals and objectives can transform difficult dialogues into more constructive and successful interactions.

One of the primary benefits of setting clear goals and objectives in challenging conversations is that it provides focus and direction. When we enter a challenging conversation without a clear sense of what we hope to achieve, we risk meandering through the discussion, getting lost in emotional turmoil, or veering off-topic. Without defined goals, it becomes challenging to keep the conversation on track and work toward a resolution.

For example, imagine a workplace scenario where an employee needs to address ongoing conflicts with a colleague. Without clear goals, the conversation might devolve into a rehash of past grievances or an unproductive blame game. However, by setting a goal such as "to reach a mutual understanding of the problems and identify concrete steps for improving collaboration," the conversation gains a sense of purpose and direction. This goal guides the participants toward a productive discussion focused on loo king forsolutions rather than dwelling on problems.

Moreover, setting clear goals and objectives in challenging conversations can help manage emotions and maintain composure. Emotions often run high in difficult discussions, leading to impulsive reactions, defensiveness, or escalation of conflicts. Having well- defined goals allows individuals to stay grounded and focused on the desired outcomes, reducing the likelihood of being swept away by intense emotions.

In a family setting, for instance, a parent might need to discuss their teenager's academic performance. Without clear objectives, this conversation could quickly escalate into an emotional argument. However, if the parent's goal is to "establish open communication with the teenager about their challenges at school and jointly develop a plan for improvement," it provides a framework for a more constructive dialogue. This goal encourages active listening, empathy, and cooperation rather than emotional outbursts.

Furthermore, clear goals and objectives enhance accountability in challenging conversations. They establish a framework for measuring progress and success. Without such benchmarks, it's challenging to determine whether the conversation is moving in the right direction or if participants are making meaningful contributions to the discussion. Setting specific objectives ensures that each participant's responsibilities and commitments are clearly defined.

For instance, in a business negotiation, parties may set the goal of "reaching a mutually beneficial agreement within one month." This goal not only provides a clear timeline but also emphasizes the shared responsibility for achieving the agreement. It encourages all parties to actively engage in problem-solving and compromise to meet the deadline.

Additionally, setting clear goals in challenging conversations promotes effective communication. Goals serve as a common point of reference, ensuring that all participants are on the same page regarding the purpose and expectations of the conversation. This shared understanding minimizes miscommunication, reduces the likelihood of misunderstandings, and fosters a more productive exchange of ideas and perspectives.

In a context where a couple is discussing financial issues, having a goal like "to create a budget that meets both partners' financial goals and responsibilities" ensures that both individuals are aligned in their purpose. It provides a clear framework for discussing income, expenses, and financial priorities, allowing for more effective communication and problem-solving.

Moreover, setting clear goals and objectives in challenging conversations encourages active participation and engagement. Participants are more likely to be invested in the discussion when they understand the specific outcomes they are working toward. This engagement promotes a sense of ownership and commitment to the conversation, increasing the likelihood of a successful outcome.

In a team meeting addressing workplace conflicts, for instance, setting the goal of "to identify common areas of disagreement and collaboratively develop strategies for resolving conflicts respectfully and constructively" encourages team members to actively contribute their insights and ideas. It transforms the conversation into a collaborative problem-solving session, where individuals actively engage in finding solutions rather than passively listening or avoiding participation.

Furthermore, clear goals and objectives empower individuals to navigate difficult conversations with confidence. When participants know what they want to achieve and how they plan to achieve it, they are better equipped to express their needs, assert their perspectives, and advocate for their interests. This empowerment fosters assertiveness and self-assuredness in challenging conversations.

For instance, in a healthcare setting, a patient may need to have a difficult conversation with their doctor about treatment options. By setting a goal such as "to gain a comprehensive understanding of available treatment choices and make an informed decision about my healthcare," the patient is equipped to engage in the conversation with a sense of agency. This goal empowers them to ask questions, seek clarification, and actively engage in the decision-making process.

In conclusion, setting precise goals and objectives is a powerful strategy for navigating challenging conversations effectively. Clear goals provide focus, direction, and purpose in discussions, ensuring that participants remain on track and work toward desired outcomes. They also help manage emotions, maintain composure, and promote accountability. Furthermore, clear goals enhance communication, encourage active engagement, and empower individuals to navigate difficult conversations with confidence. Whether in professional or personal contexts, the practice of setting clear goals and objectives transforms challenging dialogues into opportunities for productive communication, conflict resolution, and positive outcomes. So, the next time you find yourself facing a challenging conversation, take a moment to define your goals, and let them guide you toward a more constructive and successful interaction.

Gathering information and context

Navigating challenging conversations is an intricate process that requires careful consideration and strategic planning. One critical aspect of preparing for such discussions is gathering relevant information and context. Whether you are addressing conflicts at work, discussing sensitive issues with loved ones, or confronting difficult individuals, having a thorough understanding of the situation is crucial for achieving successful outcomes. In this section, we will explore the importance of gathering information and context in dealing with challenging conversations and how it can lead to more effective communication and resolution.

First and foremost, gathering information and context provides a solid foundation for productive discussions. It allows individuals to enter the conversation with a clear understanding of the facts, circumstances, and perspectives involved. Without this foundation, discussions can be marred by misunderstandings, misinterpretations, or inaccuracies, making it difficult to achieve resolution or common ground.

For example, consider a workplace scenario where a manager needs to address a team member's declining performance. Gathering information about the employee's recent work history, challenges they may be facing, and their perspective on the situation is essential. Without this context, the manager might jump to conclusions or make assumptions about the employee's motivations, potentially exacerbating the issue. With the right information, the manager can approach the conversation with empathy and a better grasp of the underlying causes, leading to a more productive discussion.

Furthermore, gathering information and context helps individuals anticipate possible challenges and objections that may arise during a challenging conversation. By understanding the different perspectives and concerns of those involved, individuals can better prepare their responses and strategies for addressing these challenges effectively. This proactive approach can prevent conversations from derailing into unproductive arguments or conflicts.

In a family setting, for instance, if parents need to discuss a change in household rules with their children, gathering information about the children's viewpoints and concerns beforehand can be invaluable. It enables the parents to anticipate objections and prepare responses that address their children's concerns while still achieving the desired outcome. This proactive approach fosters cooperation and understanding in the family dynamic.

Moreover, gathering information and context fosters empathy and understanding in challenging conversations. When individuals take the time to learn about each other's perspectives, feelings, and motivations, it creates a foundation for empathy and mutual respect. Understanding the underlying emotions and reasons behind someone's behavior or viewpoint can significantly reduce tension and promote more compassionate communication.

In a personal relationship, such as a romantic partnership, when one partner needs to address a sensitive issue with the other, gathering information about their partner's feelings and experiences related to the topic can be transformative. It allows for a deeper understanding of the emotional context, fostering empathy and creating a safe space for open and honest dialogue.

Additionally, gathering information and context helps individuals tailor their communication approach to the specific situation and audience. Not all challenging conversations are alike, and what works in one context may not be effective in another. Having a comprehensive understanding of the context, the individuals involved, and their communication styles allows individuals to adapt their approach to better suit the circumstances.

For example, when a supervisor needs to provide feedback to an employee about a mistake, gathering information about the employee's preferred communication style can be valuable. Some employees may prefer direct and straightforward feedback, while others may require a more empathetic and collaborative approach. Knowing this information allows the supervisor to communicate in a manner that is most likely to resonate with the employee and lead to a positive outcome.

Furthermore, gathering information and context can help identify potential solutions or compromises in challenging conversations. When individuals have a comprehensive understanding of the situation and the needs and interests of all parties involved, it becomes easier to brainstorm creative solutions that address everyone's concerns. This collaborative problem-solving approach can result in a more mutually beneficial outcomes.
In a business negotiation, for instance, when two parties are discussing a contract, gathering information about each party's priorities, constraints, and desired outcomes is crucial. With this context in mind, the negotiation can focus on looking for solutions that meet both parties' needs, rather than devolving into a contentious battle over conflicting interests.

Additionally, gathering information and context enables individuals to approach challenging conversations with a more open mind. It encourages a willingness to listen actively and consider alternative viewpoints. When individuals are well-informed and receptive to new information, it creates an environment where constructive dialogue can flourish.

In a community setting, such as a neighborhood association meeting to discuss a contentious issue, gathering information about the concerns and ideas of all residents fosters a more inclusive and collaborative conversation. It encourages residents to listen to each other's perspectives and explore potential compromises, ultimately leading to more harmonious community relationships.

In conclusion, gathering information and context is a vital component of successfully navigating challenging conversations. It provides a solid foundation for productive discussions, helps anticipate challenges and objections, fosters empathy and understanding, allows for tailored communication approaches, and facilitates collaborative problem-solving. Whether in personal relationships, workplace interactions, or community discussions, the practice of gathering information and context empowers individuals to approach challenging conversations with the knowledge and skills necessary to achieve positive outcomes. So, the next time you find yourself facing a challenging conversation, take the time to gather information and context—it can make all the difference in achieving a successful and constructive dialogue.

CHAPTER III

Essential Communication Skills

Active listening techniques

Building meaningful relationships—both personally and professionally—begins with effective communication. Active listening, as a fundamental component of communication, plays a pivotal role in understanding others, resolving conflicts, and fostering trust and empathy. Active listening is not just hearing words; it involves engaging fully with the speaker and demonstrating a genuine interest in their message. In this section, we will explore the importance of active listening and discuss various techniques that can enhance this essential skill.

Active listening is the art of completely focusing on the speaker, not just hearing their words but also understanding their emotions, perspectives, and needs. It requires the listener to be fully present in the moment, putting aside distractions and preconceptions to give the speaker their undivided attention. Active listening goes beyond the passive act of hearing; it involves responding to the speaker in a way that validates their feelings and encourages open communication.

Keeping eye contact is one of the fundamentals of active listening. Eye contact not only conveys respect and attentiveness but also helps the listener gauge the speaker's emotions and sincerity. When we look into someone's eyes while they speak, it sends a message that we are actively engaged in the conversation, creating an atmosphere of trust and connection.

Another essential aspect of active listening is providing verbal and nonverbal feedback. This includes nodding to show understanding, using verbal cues like "I see," "I understand," or "Tell me more," and mirroring the speaker's emotions through facial expressions and body language. Verbal and nonverbal feedback reassures the speaker that their message is being heard and understood, which is essential for effective communication.

Furthermore, active listening involves avoiding interrupting or imposing one's thoughts and opinions on the speaker. Allowing the speaker to express themselves completely without interruption demonstrates respect and patience. It also encourages them to share more openly and honestly. Interrupting or immediately offering solutions can stifle communication and make the speaker feel unheard or dismissed.

In challenging conversations or conflict resolution, paraphrasing and summarizing are valuable active listening techniques. Paraphrasing involves restating the speaker's message in your own words, demonstrating that you are actively processing their thoughts and feelings. Summarizing, on the other hand, involves briefly recapping the key points of the conversation, helping both the speaker and the listener stay on track and ensuring that important details are not overlooked.

Empathy is a central component of active listening. It involves not only understanding the speaker's perspective but also genuinely feeling their emotions. Empathy is the ability to put oneself in the speaker's shoes, to connect on an emotional level, and to convey that understanding. It often involves using phrases like "I can imagine that must be difficult" or "I'm here for you, and I care about how you feel."

Silence is another powerful active listening tool. While it may seem counterintuitive, moments of silence during a conversation can provide space for the speaker to gather their thoughts and express themselves more fully. Silence also allows the listener to reflect on what has been said and to formulate thoughtful responses. It is essential to be comfortable with pauses in the conversation rather than rushing to fill them.

Active listening can also be enhanced by asking open-ended questions. Open-ended questions invite the speaker to elaborate and provide more information, leading to a deeper and more meaningful conversation. Examples of open-ended questions include "Can you tell me more about that?" or "How do you feel about the situation?"

Furthermore, active listening involves suspending judgment and avoiding making assumptions about the speaker's intentions or motivations. Instead, the listener approaches the conversation with an open mind, seeking to understand the speaker's perspective without preconceived notions. Suspending judgment allows for more constructive and empathetic communication.

Reflective listening is another technique that involves reflecting the speaker's feelings and thoughts back to them. For example, if a friend is expressing frustration about a challenging project at work, you might say, "It sounds like you're feeling overwhelmed by the project's demands." Reflective listening validates the speaker's emotions and helps them feel heard and understood.

Active listening techniques can be particularly valuable in conflict resolution. When conflicts arise, emotions often run high, and effective communication becomes even more critical. Active listening in conflict situations involves creating a safe and nonjudgmental space for each party to express their grievances and concerns fully.

For example, if two coworkers are in conflict over a project, an active listener might say, "I want to hear both of your perspectives on this issue without interruption. Let's start with one person speaking while the other listens, and then we'll switch." This approach ensures that both parties have the opportunity to express themselves and feel heard.

In conclusion, strong relationships and effective communication both depend on the critical skill of active listening. It involves fully engaging with the speaker, maintaining eye contact, providing verbal and nonverbal feedback, avoiding interruptions, and demonstrating empathy. Paraphrasing, summarizing, and asking open-ended questions enhance active listening, as does the use of reflective listening techniques. Active listening is particularly valuable in conflict resolution, where it creates a safe and respectful environment for parties to express their concerns and work toward mutually beneficial solutions. By honing active listening skills, individuals can enhance their communication abilities and build deeper and more meaningful connections with others. So, the next time you find yourself in a conversation, keep in mind the power of active listening to facilitate understanding and create stronger bonds with those around you.

Non-verbal communication cues

Communication is a multifaceted process that extends beyond words and spoken language. Non-verbal communication cues, which encompass body language, facial expressions, gestures, and the tone of voice, play a pivotal part in conveying information, emotions, and intentions. These cues often speak louder than words, influencing how others perceive and interpret our messages. In this section, we will explore the significance of non-verbal communication cues, their various forms, and their impact on effective communication and interpersonal relationships. Non-verbal communication cues are an integral in human interaction. They complement verbal communication by providing additional context and nuance to our messages. In fact, studies suggest that non-verbal cues can account for a notable part of the overall meaning conveyed in a communication exchange. For example, a warm smile and enthusiastic tone of voice can convey happiness and genuine interest, even when the words spoken are relatively neutral.

One of the most noticeable forms of non-verbal communication is body language. Our posture, gestures, and movements communicate a wealth of information about our emotions, intentions, and level of engagement. For instance, slouched shoulders and crossed arms may indicate defensiveness or resistance, while an upright posture and open gestures convey attentiveness and receptiveness.

Facial expressions are another powerful non-verbal communication cue. The human face can express an array of emotions, from surprise and joy to anger and sadness. The muscles in our face contract and relax in response to our emotional experiences, allowing others to perceive and empathize with our feelings. A genuine smile, for example, is characterized by the contraction of muscles around the eyes and mouth and is universally recognized as a sign of happiness and warmth.

Tone of voice is yet another crucial non-verbal cue that conveys emotions and intentions. The way we speak—whether our voice is cheerful, monotonous, soothing, or agitated—can profoundly influence how our words are received. A calm and reassuring tone can help diffuse tension in a difficult conversation, while a harsh or sarcastic tone may escalate conflicts.

Gestures also play a significant role in non-verbal communication. They can complement and reinforce verbal messages or convey information independently.

For example, pointing can indicate direction or emphasis, while waving can signal greeting or farewell. Some gestures are culturally specific and may carry different meanings in various parts of the world, highlighting the importance of cultural awareness in non-verbal communication.

Eye contact is a non-verbal cue that holds particular significance in communication. It can convey interest, attentiveness, and confidence. However, the appropriate level of eye contact can vary across cultures, with some cultures valuing prolonged eye contact as a symbol of sincerity and others viewing it as intrusive or disrespectful. Effective communicators are mindful of cultural differences and adapt their eye contact accordingly.

Proximity, or personal space, is yet another dimension of non-verbal communication. The distance we maintain between ourselves and others during a conversation can signal our comfort level and the nature of our relationship. For example, standing too close to someone may be perceived as invasive, while maintaining too much distance can convey disinterest or coldness. Understanding and respecting personal space boundaries is essential for effective communication.

Touch is a powerful non-verbal cue that can convey an array of emotions and intentions. A warm handshake can signal friendliness and trust, while a pat on the back can convey encouragement and support. However, the appropriateness of touch varies greatly depending on cultural standards and the nature of the relationship. Some individuals may be uncomfortable with physical contact, emphasizing the importance of respecting boundaries.

Non-verbal cues also play a critical role in building rapport and trust in interpersonal relationships. When our non-verbal cues align with our verbal messages, they create a sense of congruence and authenticity. In contrast, incongruent cues, where verbal and non-verbal messages conflict, can lead to confusion and distrust. For example, if someone offers a verbal apology with a smirk on their face, the sincerity of their apology may be questioned.

Moreover, non-verbal communication cues are particularly influential in emotional situations. During moments of grief, joy, anger, or excitement, our non-verbal cues often reveal the depth and authenticity of our emotions. A tight hug, tears of joy, or clenched fists can convey emotions more powerfully than words alone. Empathetic individuals are skilled at recognizing and responding to these non-verbal cues to provide emotional support and understanding.

Non-verbal communication cues are also crucial in the realm of leadership and influence. Effective leaders are adept at using non-verbal cues to inspire and motivate their teams. A leader's body language, facial expressions, and tone of voice can convey confidence, enthusiasm, and a sense of purpose, instilling trust and confidence in their vision and decisions. Conversely, leaders who display incongruent or negative non-verbal cues may undermine their credibility and influence.

In the context of conflict resolution and negotiation, non-verbal cues can either facilitate or hinder productive communication. Active listening, as exemplified by attentive body language, eye contact, and open gestures, can signal a willingness to understand and collaborate. Conversely, defensive or aggressive non-verbal cues, such as crossed arms, raised voices, or pointed fingers, can escalate conflicts and impede resolution.

In conclusion, non-verbal communication cues are an integral aspect of human interaction, complementing and enhancing verbal messages. They convey emotions, intentions, and nuances that words alone cannot capture. Understanding and using non-verbal cues effectively can lead to more authentic and meaningful communication, fostering trust, empathy, and rapport in interpersonal relationships. Whether in personal interactions, professional settings, or cross-cultural contexts, the mastery of non-verbal communication cues is a valuable skill that improves our ability to connect, empathize, and influence others effectively. So, the next time you engage in a conversation, remember that words are just one part of the equation—your non-verbal cues may be conveying just as much, if not more, than what you say.

Effective questioning and probing

In order to be effective, communication must be a dynamic process that actively seeks understanding and insight in addition to sharing information. At the heart of this process lies the art of asking questions and probing for deeper understanding. Questions are powerful tools that enable individuals to gather information, clarify ideas, and navigate complex conversations. In this section, we will delve into the importance of effective questioning and probing, the various types of questions, and how mastering these skills can enhance communication, problem-solving, and relationship- building.

Effective questioning is the art of framing and delivering questions in a way that encourages meaningful responses and fosters productive dialogue. Questions serve multiple purposes, including gathering information, exploring perspectives, and eliciting thoughtful reflection. They can open doors to deeper understanding and provide a structured framework for problem-solving and decision-making.

One of the fundamental benefits of effective questioning is that it encourages active engagement in conversations. Thoughtful questions invite individuals to participate actively, share their insights, and contribute to the exchange of ideas. This engagement not only promotes a sense of involvement but also helps prevent conversations from becoming one-sided or dominated by a single perspective.

Effective questioning is particularly valuable in professional contexts, such as meetings and interviews, where gathering information and generating ideas are essential. For instance, during a job interview, a well-crafted question can prompt the candidate to provide specific examples of their skills and experiences, offering valuable insights into their qualifications as well as suitability for the role.

Moreover, effective questioning fosters critical thinking and problem-solving. Thought-provoking questions encourage individuals to analyze, evaluate, and reflect on complex issues, leading to more informed and strategic decision-making. This skill is invaluable in a variety of settings, from academia to business, where problem-solving and decision-making are central to success.

There are various types of questions that serve different purposes in communication. Open-ended questions, for example, encourage individuals to provide detailed and reflective responses. These questions commonly begin with words like "what," "how," or "why" and invite individuals to share their thoughts, feelings, and experiences. Open-ended questions are particularly effective in exploring perspectives and encouraging in-depth discussions.

In contrast, closed-ended questions typically have a yes-or-no answer or require brief, specific responses. They are useful for gathering factual information and clarifying details. For instance, in a customer service context, a closed-ended question like "Did you receive the product on time?" can quickly ascertain whether a service met expectations.

Probing questions are a subset of open-ended questions that delve deeper into a topic or response. They are designed to encourage individuals to provide more details or explore their thoughts further. Probing questions often begin with phrases like "Can you tell me more about..." or "What led you to that conclusion?" These questions are valuable in interviews, counseling, and investigative contexts where uncovering underlying information is crucial.

Reflective questions prompt individuals to think critically about their experiences, behaviors, and decisions. They encourage self-reflection and can lead to personal insight and growth. For example, a reflective question like "What did you learn from that experience?" encourages individuals to consider the lessons they've gained from past events.

Empathetic questions convey understanding and empathy for another person's feelings or experiences. They often begin with phrases like "I can imagine that must have been challenging..." or "How did that make you feel?" Empathetic questions are important in providing emotional support and building trust in personal relationships and counseling settings.

Leading questions, on the other hand, guide individuals toward a particular response or viewpoint. They often contain implicit suggestions or assumptions that can influence the response. While leading questions can be manipulative, they are sometimes used in investigative contexts to prompt witnesses or suspects to reveal information.

Effective questioning and probing are crucial in situations that require active listening and empathy, such as counseling or conflict resolution. For instance, when helping someone navigate a personal challenge, asking empathetic and probing questions can create a safe space for them to share their feelings and thoughts. This can result in a more profound understanding of their perspective and needs.

In addition to their role in information gathering and problem-solving, questions are essential for building rapport and trust in interpersonal relationships. When individuals feel that their perspectives and opinions are valued, they are more likely to open up and share. Asking questions that show genuine interest and curiosity can strengthen connections and enhance communication in personal and professional relationships.

Furthermore, effective questioning and probing are essential in educational settings. Teachers use questions to stimulate student engagement, assess comprehension, and encourage critical thinking. Well-crafted questions can guide students in exploring complex subjects, making connections, and deepening their understanding.

In conclusion, effective questioning and probing are essential skills that underpin effective communication, critical thinking, problem-solving, and relationship-building. Questions serve as tools for gathering information, exploring perspectives, and fostering productive dialogue. By mastering the art of asking thoughtful and appropriate questions, individuals can enhance their ability to engage with others, seek understanding, and navigate complex conversations with skill and empathy. Whether in personal relationships, professional contexts, or educational settings, effective questioning and probing are powerful tools for promoting mutual understanding and facilitating more meaningful and productive interactions. So, the next time you engage in a conversation, consider the impact of your questions and the opportunities they create for deeper understanding and connection.

CHAPTER IV

Strategies for Dealing with Difficult People

The "EAR" approach (Empathize, Assert, Redirect)

Effective communication is a skill that serves as the cornerstone of healthy relationships and successful interactions. When faced with challenging conversations, the ability to navigate them with clarity, empathy, and assertiveness is invaluable. One valuable framework for approaching difficult conversations is the "EAR" approach, which stands for Empathize, Assert, and Redirect. This approach provides a structured framework for engaging in challenging dialogues, promoting understanding, and achieving positive outcomes. In this section, we will explore the components of the "EAR" approach and how it can be a potent tool for effective communication and conflict resolution.

Empathize, the first step in the "EAR" approach, involves acknowledging and understanding the emotions and perspectives of the other party. It requires actively listening and demonstrating genuine concern for their feelings and experiences. Empathy is a fundamental component of effective communication, as it creates a secure and supportive environment for the conversation. When individuals feel heard and validated, they are more likely to be open and receptive to the conversation.

Empathizing can be especially crucial in difficult conversations where emotions are running high. For instance, in a conflict with a colleague, taking a moment to empathize with their frustration or concerns can defuse tension and create an atmosphere of mutual respect. Empathizing allows individuals to connect on a human level, recognizing that emotions and reactions are valid and natural.

Empathizing can be conveyed through verbal and non-verbal cues, such as active listening, making eye contact, and using empathetic language. Phrases like "I understand how you feel" or "I can see why this is important to you" demonstrate empathy and create a sense of understanding. By starting a challenging conversation with empathy, individuals lay the foundation for constructive dialogue.

The second component of the "EAR" approach is Assert, which involves expressing one's thoughts, feelings, and needs clearly and respectfully. Assertiveness is essential in challenging conversations because it ensures that individuals communicate their perspectives and boundaries effectively. It allows them to advocate for themselves and their concerns without aggression or passivity.

Assertiveness involves using "I" statements to convey personal thoughts and feelings. For example, instead of saying, "You always interrupt me," an assertive statement might be, "I feel frustrated when I'm interrupted because it makes it hard for me to express my ideas." This approach concentrates on personal experiences and avoids placing blame on the other party, fostering a less defensive response.

Assertiveness is particularly valuable when addressing behavior that is causing harm or discomfort. Whether it's discussing boundaries in a personal relationship or addressing unprofessional conduct in the workplace, assertiveness ensures that individuals communicate their expectations and concerns clearly and assertively.

The final component of the "EAR" approach is Redirect, which involves steering the conversation toward a constructive and productive outcome. Redirecting is essential because it prevents conversations from becoming unproductive or escalating into conflicts. It involves moving the conversation away from blame, accusations, or unhelpful arguments and toward solutions or resolution.

Redirecting often involves problem-solving and focusing on actionable steps. Instead of assigning blame or dwelling on past mistakes, individuals redirect the conversation toward finding common ground, exploring alternatives, or creating a plan for moving forward. This shift in focus encourages collaboration and problem-solving rather than perpetuating negativity.

In workplace situations, for instance, if a team member consistently misses deadlines, a redirecting approach might involve saying, "Let's discuss how we can ensure that our project timelines are met in the future." This approach changes the conversation from blame to solution-oriented discussions about improving the team's workflow and accountability.

The "EAR" approach can be especially effective in situations where emotions are heightened, and there is potential for conflict. By empathizing with the other party's feelings and concerns, individuals can defuse tension and create a sense of understanding. Assertiveness ensures that they communicate their own needs and boundaries clearly, and redirection focuses the conversation on resolving the issue or finding common ground.

It's important to note that the "EAR" approach is not a one-size-fits-all solution. Its effectiveness depends on the particular context and the individuals involved. Some conversations may require more emphasis on empathy and understanding, while others may necessitate assertiveness and redirection from the outset. Skilled communicators can adapt the approach to suit the unique dynamics of each conversation.

Additionally, it's essential to practice active listening throughout the "EAR" approach. Active listening includes not only hearing the words spoken but also comprehending the emotions, intentions, and the underlying messages. It requires focused attention, empathy, and the ability to ask clarifying questions when necessary.

Moreover, the "EAR" approach is most effective when both parties are willing to engage constructively in the conversation. In some situations, the other party may not be receptive or may respond defensively. In such cases, individuals can still apply the "EAR" approach by demonstrating empathy, asserting their perspective respectfully, and attempting to redirect the conversation. However, they may need to be prepared for the possibility that the conversation may not reach a positive resolution.

In conclusion, the "EAR" approach (Empathize, Assert, Redirect) is a valuable framework for navigating challenging conversations and conflict resolution. It emphasizes the importance of empathy, assertiveness, and redirecting the conversation toward positive outcomes. By starting with empathy, individuals create a foundation of understanding and respect. Assertiveness ensures that their needs and boundaries are communicated clearly and respectfully, and redirection shifts the conversation toward problem-solving and resolution. While the "EAR" approach is not a panacea for all communication challenges, it is a powerful tool that can help individuals engage in difficult conversations with skill and effectiveness, ultimately leading to more positive outcomes and stronger relationships. So, the next time you find yourself facing a challenging conversation, consider applying the "EAR" approach to facilitate understanding, assert your needs, and redirect the conversation toward a productive outcome.

Setting boundaries and assertiveness

Dealing with difficult people is an inevitable part of life, whether it's in our personal relationships or professional endeavors. While it can be challenging, there are various strategies to effectively navigate such situations. One of the most valuable approaches is setting boundaries and practicing assertiveness. These techniques empower individuals to maintain their self-respect, protect their emotional well-being, and foster healthier interactions with challenging personalities.

Setting boundaries is a fundamental aspect of interpersonal relationships. Boundaries are like invisible lines that define what is acceptable and unacceptable behavior from others. When dealing with difficult people, it becomes crucial to establish clear and consistent boundaries. This means communicating what you will and won't tolerate in a respectful and assertive manner. By doing so, you assert control over your personal space and emotional boundaries, sending a message that your requirements and feelings are valid and deserving of respect.

Moreover, setting boundaries is not about creating walls or isolating oneself from difficult individuals. It is about striking a balance between self-preservation and maintaining a connection. Boundaries can encompass physical, emotional, and even time-related aspects. For instance, if someone is consistently disrespectful or intrusive, you can establish an emotional boundary by calmly but firmly letting them know that their behavior is unacceptable and won't be tolerated.

Assertiveness is closely linked to setting boundaries and plays a pivotal role in dealing with difficult people. Being assertive means expressing your feelings, thoughts, and needs clearly and respectfully while standing up for yourself without being aggressive or passive. It is a communication style that permits individuals to advocate for their interests and maintain their dignity in challenging interactions.

Assertiveness empowers individuals to assert their boundaries effectively. When faced with a difficult person, assertive communication can help you address the issue directly. For example, if a colleague consistently takes credit for your ideas, you can assertively communicate your concerns by saying, "I've noticed that you've been taking credit for my work during our team meetings, and I find it unfair. I would appreciate it if you give credit where it's due."

One of the key advantages of assertiveness is that it fosters open and honest communication. It encourages the difficult person to see your perspective and engage in a constructive dialogue, rather than becoming defensive or escalating the conflict. This approach often leads to a more positive and collaborative resolution, as both parties can express their needs and worries without resorting to aggression or passive-aggression.

Furthermore, assertiveness helps individuals maintain their self-esteem and confidence in challenging situations. When dealing with difficult people, it's common for one's self-esteem to take a hit due to constant criticism or manipulation. However, assertiveness allows you to defend your self-worth and ensure that your feelings are acknowledged and respected. By expressing your needs and boundaries assertively, you send a powerful message that you deserve to be treated with respect and consideration.

In addition to self-preservation, assertiveness also promotes empathy and understanding. It allows difficult individuals to gain insight into the impact of their behavior on others. When you assertively communicate your feelings and boundaries, you provide them with an opportunity to reflect on their actions and possibly change their behavior. This can be particularly valuable in personal relationships where maintaining the connection is important, but problematic behavior needs to be addressed.

It's important to note that assertiveness is a skill that can be learned and practiced. Many people struggle with assertiveness because they fear confrontation or believe that being passive is the path of least resistance. However, by developing assertiveness skills, individuals can become more effective in dealing with difficult people while maintaining their emotional well-being.

Another aspect of setting boundaries and assertiveness is learning to say "no" when necessary. Difficult people often exploit those who are unable to decline their requests or demands. By confidently and assertively saying "no" when it's appropriate, you establish your boundaries and protect your time and energy. This doesn't mean you should be inflexible or uncooperative, but rather that you should prioritize your own needs and responsibilities.

Saying "no" assertively can be challenging, especially when you're accustomed to accommodating others. However, it is a crucial skill for maintaining personal and professional balance. For example, if a friend consistently asks for favors that inconvenience you, saying, "I'm sorry, but I can't help you with that this time because I have other commitments," is an assertive way to decline without compromising your boundaries.

Moreover, setting boundaries and practicing assertiveness are essential for preventing emotional burnout and stress when dealing with difficult people. Constantly tolerating unacceptable behavior or suppressing your feelings can lead to increased frustration, resentment, and emotional exhaustion. By asserting your boundaries and communicating your needs, you take proactive steps to safeguard your mental and emotional well-being.

In the workplace, setting boundaries and practicing assertiveness can be particularly beneficial for job satisfaction and career growth. Difficult colleagues or superiors can hinder productivity and create a toxic work environment. However, by setting clear boundaries and asserting yourself when necessary, you can mitigate the negative impact of such individuals on your professional life. This not only helps you maintain a sense of control but can also earn you respect from colleagues and superiors who value assertive and principled individuals. In conclusion, setting boundaries and practicing assertiveness are indispensable strategies for dealing with difficult people. These techniques empower individuals to protect their self-respect, emotional well-being, and personal boundaries. By communicating assertively and establishing clear boundaries, you can maintain healthier interactions, foster empathy and understanding, and ultimately create more positive and constructive relationships with even the most challenging individuals. While it may require practice and effort, the benefits of these strategies in both personal and professional spheres make them invaluable tools for navigating the complexities of human interactions.

Handling aggressive and passive-aggressive behavior

Dealing with difficult people is a skill that is often essential in both personal and professional life. Among the various strategies available, effectively handling aggressive and passive-aggressive behavior is crucial. Aggressive and passive-aggressive individuals can be challenging to interact with, but with the right approach, one can navigate these situations with confidence and composure, ultimately fostering better relationships and minimizing conflict.

Aggressive behavior in difficult people can manifest in various ways, including verbal attacks, threats, and physical intimidation. When confronted with aggression, it's important to remember that your safety and well- being are paramount. In situations where physical security is a concern, seeking immediate help or removing yourself from the situation is crucial. However, in most cases, dealing with verbal aggression is more common.

One effective strategy for handling aggressive behavior is to remain calm and composed. Aggressive individuals often try to provoke a reaction or engage in power struggles. By maintaining your emotional equilibrium, you can disrupt this dynamic. Responding to aggression with aggression typically escalates the situation and rarely leads to a positive outcome.

Active listening is another valuable technique when dealing with aggressive individuals. Give them an opportunity to express themselves, even if their communication is hostile. This not only shows respect for their perspective but also allows them to release pent-up frustration. Once they have had a chance to speak, you can assertively respond, addressing their concerns and, if necessary, setting boundaries for acceptable behavior. Setting boundaries is particularly important when dealing with aggressive individuals. Clearly and assertively communicate your limits and expectations, making it known that you will not tolerate disrespectful or aggressive behavior. For instance, if a colleague raises their voice during a meeting, you can calmly state, "I'm willing to discuss this matter, but I expect our conversation to remain respectful and free from shouting."

Additionally, avoid getting drawn into an argument or power struggle. Aggressive individuals often thrive on confrontation and may attempt to engage you in a battle of words. Instead, focus on finding common ground or seeking a resolution to the issue at hand. If the situation becomes unbearable or unproductive, it may be necessary to involve a mediator or supervisor to facilitate a more productive conversation.

On the other end of the spectrum, passive-aggressive behavior can be equally frustrating and challenging to handle. Passive-aggressive individuals often express their hostility or resistance indirectly, making it difficult to address the issue head-on. They may use sarcasm, backhanded compliments, or subtle forms of sabotage to convey their dissatisfaction.

When dealing with passive-aggressive behavior, it's essential to recognize the signs and not dismiss them as mere misunderstandings. Addressing passive-aggressiveness requires patience and a commitment to open communication.

One strategy is to ask for clarification. When you suspect passive-aggressive behavior, instead of reacting defensively, inquire about the person's true feelings or intentions. For example, if someone consistently cancels plans at the last minute, you can calmly ask, "I've noticed that you often cancel our plans. Is there something bothering you that you'd like to discuss?"

Effective communication is key to addressing passive-aggressive behavior. Encourage open as well as honest conversations where both parties can express their feelings as well as concerns. Express your own feelings and observations without accusations, and encourage the other person to do the same. This approach can help uncover the underlying issues that may be driving the passive-aggressive behavior.

Setting clear expectations and boundaries is also crucial when dealing with passive-aggressive individuals. Make it known that you value open and direct communication and that passive-aggressive tactics are not an acceptable means of addressing problems. By establishing these boundaries, you create a framework for healthier interactions.

Furthermore, avoid becoming passive-aggressive in response to their behavior. It's easy to get caught in a cycle of passive-aggressive exchanges, which only perpetuates the problem. Instead, model assertive communication by addressing the issue directly and expressing your feelings in a straightforward manner. In both cases of aggressive and passive-aggressive behavior, it's essential to practice empathy and active listening. Try to understand the underlying emotions or motives driving the difficult person's behavior. They may be dealing with stress, insecurity, or personal issues that are influencing their actions. By acknowledging their feelings, you can create a more empathetic and less confrontational atmosphere. It's important to remember that handling aggressive and passive-aggressive behavior is not about changing the difficult person but about managing your own reactions and responses. You cannot control how others behave, but you can control the way you react to their behavior. By staying composed, setting boundaries, and fostering open communication, you can effectively navigate these challenging situations while maintaining your own emotional well-being.

In conclusion, dealing with aggressive and passive-aggressive behavior is an essential skill for effectively managing difficult people. By remaining calm, practicing active listening, and setting clear boundaries, you can address aggressive behavior assertively and prevent escalation. When dealing with passive-aggressive individuals, open and empathetic communication is key to uncovering the underlying issues and fostering healthier interactions. While it can be challenging, mastering these strategies can lead to a more harmonious relationships and reduced conflict with even the most difficult personalities in your life.

CHAPTER V

Case Studies and Real-Life Examples

Real-world scenarios and how to handle them

Difficult people are an inevitable part of life, and navigating challenging interactions can be both stressful and draining. However, by understanding various real- world scenarios and employing effective strategies, individuals can develop the skills necessary to handle these situations with grace as well as confidence. In this section, we will explore several common scenarios involving difficult people and offer guidance on how to handle them.

Scenario 1: The Overly Critical Colleague

In the workplace, it's not uncommon to encounter a colleague who consistently criticizes your work or undermines your contributions. Handling such a situation requires a blend of assertiveness and diplomacy. Start by actively listening to their feedback, and if their criticism is valid, acknowledge it and express your willingness to improve. However, if their criticism is unfounded or excessive, calmly and assertively communicate your perspective. You can say something like, "I appreciate your feedback, but I believe my approach aligns with our project goals. Let's discuss how we can work together more effectively." This approach demonstrates your professionalism and also willingness to collaborate while setting boundaries against unwarranted criticism.

Scenario 2: The Manipulative Friend

Dealing with a manipulative friend can be emotionally draining. Such friends may use guilt, emotional blackmail, or passive-aggressive tactics to control or manipulate you. In this scenario, it's crucial to prioritize your well-being and maintain healthy boundaries. Politely but firmly assert your boundaries and express your feelings. For instance, if a friend is constantly asking for favors that inconvenience you, you can say, "I value our friendship, but I need to prioritize my own commitments right now." Be prepared for pushback, but remain steadfast in your boundaries to protect your emotional health.

Scenario 3: The Aggressive Customer

Customer service roles often involve dealing with aggressive or irate customers. In these situations, it's essential to remain calm and empathetic while addressing the issue. Listen actively to the customer's concerns, and acknowledge their feelings, even if you don't agree with them. Offer solutions or alternatives to address the issue, and maintain a professional and respectful demeanor. If the customer becomes abusive or unreasonable, it may be necessary to involve a supervisor or manager to ensure their concerns are addressed appropriately.

Scenario 4: The Passive-Aggressive Co-worker

Passive-aggressive co-workers can create a toxic work environment with their subtle forms of resistance and hostility. When confronted with passive-aggressive behavior, address it directly but tactfully. Ask for clarification about their intentions, such as saying, "I've noticed some tension between us. Is there something specific you'd like to discuss or address?" Encourage open and honest communication, and express your desire for a more collaborative and respectful working relationship.

Scenario 5: The Disruptive Team Member

In group settings, disruptive team members can hinder progress and cohesion. Whether it's a classmate, a colleague, or a fellow volunteer, addressing disruptive behavior is crucial for the success of the team. Start by having a private conversation with the disruptive individual to understand their perspective and motivations. Express your concerns and the impact of their behavior on the group. Collaboratively brainstorm solutions or ways to modify their behavior to better align with the team's goals. If the issue persists, involve a supervisor or authority figure to mediate and enforce necessary consequences.

Scenario 6: The Difficult Family Member

Dealing with a challenging family member can be emotionally charged and complex. In these situations, boundaries, empathy, and effective communication are key. Establish clear boundaries to safeguard your emotional well-being and communicate your expectations calmly but assertively. Seek to understand their perspective and motivations, and express your own feelings without judgment. Consider involving a family therapist or mediator to facilitate more productive discussions and help the family member address their behavior.

Scenario 7: The Condescending Boss

A condescending boss can create a challenging work environment and impact job satisfaction. When dealing with a condescending superior, focus on maintaining your professionalism and self-respect. Seek private conversations to express your concerns about their communication style and its impact on your performance. Use "I" statements to convey your feelings and observations, such as "I feel demotivated when I'm spoken to in a condescending manner." Document instances of condescension if necessary, and consider discussing the issue with HR or higher management if the behavior persists.

Scenario 8: The Argumentative Neighbor

Living in close proximity to an argumentative neighbor can lead to ongoing tension and conflict. In these situations, prioritize open communication and conflict resolution. Strike up a discussion with your neighbor about how much you'd like to live in harmony. After you have gained an understanding of their worries and emotions through active listening, gently offer your own viewpoint. Explore potential compromises or solutions to the issues at hand, and consider involving a mediator or homeowners' association if necessary to reach a mutually agreeable resolution.

Scenario 9: The Jealous Co-worker

Jealousy among co-workers can lead to gossip, tension, and a hostile work environment. Addressing jealousy requires a delicate approach that emphasizes collaboration and support. Acknowledge your co-worker's accomplishments and express your desire for a positive working relationship. If their jealousy continues to be a problem, suggest opportunities for collaboration and emphasize the benefits of teamwork. Encourage open communication and focus on building a more supportive and cooperative work environment.

Scenario 10: The Dismissive Partner

In romantic relationships, a dismissive partner can make you feel unheard and undervalued. It's essential to assert your needs and communicate your feelings openly but calmly. Express your desire for a more attentive and respectful partnership, using "I" statements to avoid blame or accusations. Seek couples counseling if necessary to address deeper issues and improve communication within the relationship.

In conclusion, dealing with difficult people in real-world scenarios requires a combination of assertiveness, empathy, and effective communication. By recognizing the dynamics at play and employing these strategies, individuals can navigate challenging interactions with confidence and composure. Whether it's a colleague, friend, customer, family member, or neighbor, the ability to handle difficult people effectively can lead to healthier relationships, reduced conflict, and a more harmonious life.

Success stories of resolving conflicts with difficult people

Conflict resolution is an essential skill in personal and professional life. While dealing with difficult people can be challenging, there are countless success stories where individuals have effectively resolved conflicts and transformed difficult relationships into positive ones. These stories serve as valuable lessons and inspiration for anyone facing similar challenges. This section will explore a few success stories of resolving conflicts with difficult people and the strategies that contributed to these achievements.

Story 1: The Workplace Dispute

In a corporate setting, Sarah found herself embroiled in a conflict with a colleague named Mark. Mark was known for his abrasive communication style and a habit of taking credit for others' work. Initially, Sarah responded with frustration, but she recognized the need for a more constructive approach. She decided to engage in a one-on-one conversation with Mark to address the issue.

Sarah approached the conversation with a mindset of understanding rather than confrontation. She actively listened to Mark's concerns and frustrations, allowing him to express his perspective fully. As Mark spoke, it became clear that he felt undervalued and overlooked by the team. Sarah empathized with his feelings and acknowledged his contributions.

Next, Sarah expressed her own feelings and concerns, using "I" statements to avoid sounding accusatory. She mentioned specific instances where her work had been attributed to Mark and how it affected her job satisfaction. Mark, surprisingly, admitted that he had been acting defensively due to perceived threats to his job security.

Together, they brainstormed solutions to improve collaboration and communication within the team. They decided to allocate tasks more clearly, give credit where it was due, and provide regular feedback. Sarah also suggested involving their supervisor in periodic team meetings to ensure fairness and transparency.

Over time, the relationship between Sarah and Mark improved significantly. They not only resolved their conflict but also developed a more constructive and supportive working relationship. Their success story highlights the importance of open communication, empathy, and a willingness to collaborate in conflict resolution.

Story 2: A Family Reunion Reconciliation

Family conflicts can be some of the most emotionally charged and enduring. Tom and his sister, Emily, had been estranged for several years due to a dispute over their late father's inheritance. They had barely communicated during this time, and their relationship had deteriorated.

One day, Tom received news that their mother was terminally ill and wished to see her children reconciled.

This revelation prompted Tom to reach out to Emily to attempt reconciliation. Recognizing the gravity of the situation, he put aside his pride and resentment and initiated a heartfelt conversation.

Tom began by expressing his desire to mend their relationship and apologizing for his part in their estrangement. He also acknowledged Emily's feelings and listened to her grievances without interruption. Emily, initially defensive, gradually opened up about her own perspective and the pain she had felt.

Through their conversation, it became evident that both had misunderstood each other's intentions and had been holding onto old grudges. They decided to meet in person to further discuss their issues and share their experiences.

Over time, Tom and Emily managed to heal their relationship. They worked through their differences, forgave each other, and committed to building a stronger, more supportive sibling bond. Their mother's passing, while tragic, served as a catalyst for their reconciliation. Their story underscores the power of forgiveness, empathy, and prioritizing relationships over past grievances.

Story 3: Bridging the Generational Gap

Intergenerational conflicts can be particularly challenging, as differing values and communication styles often come into play. In a community organization, Jennifer, a younger member, found herself at odds with Bill, an older and more experienced member. They clashed over how to approach fundraising efforts, causing tension within the group.

Jennifer recognized the importance of Bill's experience but felt that her ideas were being dismissed solely because of her age. Instead of resorting to confrontation, she decided to have an open and respectful conversation with Bill.

Jennifer started the conversation by expressing her appreciation for Bill's contributions to the organization and her desire to learn from his experience. She acknowledged that their generational differences had led to misunderstandings and suggested that they work together to find a common ground.

Bill, initially defensive, eventually shared his concerns about the direction of the organization and his fear of losing its traditional values. Jennifer listened attentively and proposed a compromise that would incorporate both traditional and modern approaches to fundraising.

With this compromise in place, Jennifer and Bill worked together harmoniously. They combined their strengths and learned from each other's perspectives, ultimately contributing to the organization's success. Their story illustrates the importance of respecting different viewpoints, finding common ground, and collaborating for mutual benefit.

Story 4: A Marriage Renewed

Marital conflicts can be among the most challenging to resolve, often involving deeply rooted issues and emotional wounds. Sarah and David had been married for more than a decade but found themselves drifting apart due to unresolved issues and communication breakdowns.

They decided to seek couples counseling to salvage their marriage. In therapy, they learned the importance of active listening and expressing their emotions honestly but respectfully. They were encouraged to validate each other's feelings and concerns, fostering empathy and understanding.

Over time, they worked through their conflicts and rediscovered the love and connection that had initially brought them together. Through therapy, they developed effective communication skills, a stronger emotional bond, and strategies to prevent future conflicts. Their success story demonstrates the transformative power of professional guidance, emotional vulnerability, and a commitment to the relationship.

Story 5: A Neighboring Resolution

Neighbor disputes can create ongoing tension, affecting the quality of life for all parties involved. Jane had been experiencing conflicts with her neighbor, Mr. Smith, over property boundaries and noise disturbances. The situation had escalated to the point where both were considering legal action.

However, before resorting to legal measures, Jane

decided to have a calm and respectful conversation with Mr. Smith. She initiated the discussion by expressing her desire for an amicable resolution, emphasizing their shared interest in maintaining a peaceful neighborhood.

During their conversation, Jane actively listened to Mr. Smith's concerns about property boundaries and noise. She offered solutions, such as hiring a surveyor to establish property lines and discussing quiet hours for specific activities. Mr. Smith, feeling heard and respected, was open to these suggestions.

As they implemented these solutions, the conflicts

between Jane and Mr. Smith gradually dissipated. They developed a more neighborly relationship, occasionally collaborating on community projects. Their success story illustrates the benefits of open communication, collaboration, and a commitment to resolving issues peacefully.

In conclusion, success stories of resolving conflicts with difficult people demonstrate that it is possible to transform challenging relationships into positive ones. Whether in the workplace, within families, among friends, or in communities, the principles of open communication, empathy, active listening, compromise, and a commitment to resolution are universal. These stories offer inspiration and guidance for anyone facing conflict, showing that with the right approach and mindset, even the most challenging relationships can be mended and transformed for the better.

CHAPTER VI

Emotional Intelligence and Empathy

Developing emotional intelligence

Emotional intelligence, often called EQ (Emotional Quotient), is a critical skill that plays a fundamental role in our personal and professional lives. It encompasses the ability to determine, understand, manage, and influence our own emotions while also being attuned to the emotions of others. Developing emotional intelligence is not only beneficial for building stronger relationships but also for achieving personal growth and success. In this section, we will explore the importance of emotional intelligence, its components, and strategies for its development.

Emotional intelligence is essential because it underlies our ability to relate to others effectively. It affects how we handle conflicts, navigate social situations, and make decisions. Research have indicated that people with high emotional intelligence typically perform better at work, have better relationships with others, and are happier overall.

Self-awareness is one of the essential elements of emotional intelligence. Being self-aware entails identifying and comprehending our own feelings in addition to recognizing our advantages and disadvantages. It means being in tune with our feelings and having the ability to label them accurately. When we are self-aware, we can identify our emotional triggers, biases, and patterns of behavior, which allows us to make more conscious choices in how we respond to situations.

Self-regulation is another vital aspect of emotional intelligence. It involves managing our emotions and impulses effectively. Strong self-regulation allows people to manage their frustration, anger, and anxiety, which improves their ability to think clearly and make sensible decisions under pressure. It takes practice to become self-regulatory, and methods like mindfulness, deep breathing, and relaxation exercises are common.

Emotional intelligence also includes empathy, which is the capacity to comprehend and experience another person's emotions. Empathetic individuals can tune into the emotions of those around them, which is invaluable in building strong relationships and resolving conflicts. Empathy involves active listening, asking questions to understand another person's perspective, and demonstrating compassion and support.

Effective communication is closely tied to empathy and is another essential skill for emotional intelligence. Communication involves not only expressing our thoughts and feelings but also listening attentively to others. When we communicate effectively, we convey our messages clearly, avoid misunderstandings, and create an environment where open and honest discussions can take place.

Social skills, the final component of emotional intelligence, encompass a range of abilities that help us navigate social situations successfully. These skills include conflict resolution, teamwork, leadership, and the ability to build rapport with others. Strong social skills are valuable in both personal and professional settings, as they contribute to our ability to collaborate, influence, and inspire others.

Being self-aware is the first step in the lifetime journey of developing emotional intelligence. To enhance self-awareness, individuals can start by regularly reflecting on their emotions and their triggers. Journaling, meditation, and seeking feedback from trusted friends or mentors can also be helpful in gaining deeper insight into one's emotional patterns.

Self-regulation can be developed through techniques such as mindfulness and meditation. Through these exercises, people can improve their ability to recognize and control their emotions. Learning to pause and take a step back before reacting to a situation can also be a valuable self-regulation strategy.

Empathy and effective communication can be honed through active listening and practicing perspective-taking. When engaging in conversations, make a conscious effort to truly listen to what others are saying, and avoid interrupting or formulating responses in your mind while they are speaking. Show empathy by acknowledging others' emotions and validating their feelings, even if you may not agree with their perspective.

To enhance social skills, individuals can actively seek opportunities for collaboration, leadership roles, and teamwork. Joining clubs, organizations, or volunteering can provide valuable experiences for developing and refining these skills. Additionally, seeking feedback from colleagues, supervisors, or mentors can help identify areas for improvement in social interactions.

It's worth noting that developing emotional intelligence is not a one-size-fits-all process. Each person's journey will be unique, and it may require ongoing effort and practice. However, the benefits of enhancing emotional intelligence are well worth the investment.

People who possess high emotional intelligence are often seen as valuable assets in the workplace. Their exceptional abilities in collaboration, flexibility, and handling conflict lead to a happier and more efficient workplace. Moreover, they tend to be effective leaders who can inspire and motivate their teams.

In personal relationships, emotional intelligence is the foundation of healthy and fulfilling connections. It allows individuals to communicate more openly and empathetically with their partners, friends, and family members. In times of conflict, those with strong emotional intelligence can navigate disagreements more constructively, leading to better resolutions and deeper connections.

Furthermore, emotional intelligence is closely tied to personal well-being and mental health. People with high emotional intelligence tend to experience lower levels of stress and anxiety. They are better equipped to manage their emotions, which reduces the risk of burnout and emotional exhaustion.

In conclusion, building emotional intelligence is a valuable endeavor that can significantly enhance our personal and professional lives. It involves self-awareness, self-regulation, empathy, effective communication, and social skills. By practicing self-awareness and implementing strategies for improvement, individuals can strengthen their emotional intelligence, leading to better relationships, improved decision-making, and increased overall well-being. Embracing and developing emotional intelligence is not only an investment in ourselves but also in the quality of our interactions and the success of our endeavors.

Practicing empathy in difficult conversations

Difficult conversations are an inevitable part of life, whether they occur in personal relationships or professional settings. These conversations often involve topics that are emotionally charged, sensitive, or contentious. While it's natural to approach such discussions with apprehension, practicing empathy can be a powerful tool for navigating them effectively and with greater understanding. In this section, we will explore the importance of empathy in difficult conversations, how it can be cultivated and applied, and the transformative impact it can have on the outcomes of these conversations.

The capacity to understand and experience another person's emotions is known as empathy. It involves stepping into someone else's shoes, seeing the world from their perspective, and recognizing their emotions without judgment. In difficult conversations, empathy serves as a bridge that connects individuals, fostering mutual understanding and creating a secure space for open and honest communication.

The first step in practicing empathy in difficult conversations is to actively listen. Giving the speaker your undivided attention while they are speaking and not forming an answer during their speech is known as active listening. Even if you disagree with the speaker's point of view, you must be patient and open to understanding it. By actively listening, you signal to the other person that their perspective is valued and respected.

Empathetic listening also involves asking open-ended questions and seeking clarification. Allow the other person to elaborate on their ideas and emotions. For example, you can say, "Tell me more about how you're feeling" or "Help me understand why this is important to you." By inviting them to share, you demonstrate your genuine interest in their perspective.

Nonverbal cues are essential in conveying empathy as well. Maintain eye contact, use affirmative gestures like nodding, and adopt an open and relaxed posture to signal your receptivity. Nonverbal cues can communicate your empathy and sincerity more effectively than words alone.

Empathy also requires the ability to validate the other person's feelings. Acknowledge their emotions and let them know that what they are experiencing is valid and understandable. For example, you can say, "I can see that this situation is really upsetting for you, and I can understand why."

Another crucial aspect of empathy is withholding judgment. In difficult conversations, it's common for people to have differing opinions, beliefs, or values. While you may not agree with the other person's perspective, empathy entails suspending judgment and refraining from criticizing or condemning them. Instead, focus on understanding their viewpoint and the underlying emotions driving it.

Cultivating empathy in difficult conversations often begins with self-awareness. Reflect on your biases, assumptions, and emotional triggers that may influence your responses. Recognizing your own emotional reactions and learning to manage them can help you approach conversations with a more open and empathetic mindset.

Additionally, practicing empathy requires a willingness to be vulnerable. Share your own feelings and experiences when appropriate, as this can create a more reciprocal and empathetic exchange. However, be mindful not to make the conversation about yourself; the goal is still to understand and support the other person.

Empathy also involves being patient and giving the other person time to express themselves fully. In difficult conversations, emotions may run high, and it may take time for the other person to articulate their thoughts and feelings. Be patient, and endure the urge to rush or interrupt them.

Moreover, empathy entails managing your own emotional reactions. Should the discourse turn tense or emotionally charged, it's essential to remain calm and composed. Responding with anger or defensiveness can hinder empathy and escalate the conflict. Practice emotional self-regulation strategies, such as deep breathing or taking a brief break if needed, to maintain your composure.

The benefits of practicing empathy in difficult conversations are manifold. First and foremost, it facilitates better communication and understanding. When people feel heard and validated, they are more likely to open up and share their genuine thoughts and feelings. This, in turn, can lead to more productive and constructive discussions.

Empathy also builds trust and strengthens relationships. When individuals perceive that you genuinely care about their feelings and perspectives, they are more likely to trust your intentions and cooperate in finding solutions to the issues at hand. Trust is a fondation of healthy relationships, and empathy plays a significant role in its cultivation.

Additionally, practicing empathy can lead to more effective conflict resolution. In difficult conversations, conflicts often arise due to miscommunications, misunderstandings, or differing viewpoints. Empathy helps uncover the root causes of conflicts and allows for more creative problem-solving. When both parties feel heard and valued, they will likely work together to find mutually agreeable solutions.

Moreover, empathy can diffuse tension and reduce defensiveness. When people perceive that you are genuinely trying to understand their perspective, they are less likely to become defensive or hostile. This creates a more emotionally safe environment for discussing sensitive topics.

In professional settings, empathy can lead to improved teamwork, enhanced leadership, and better workplace relationships. Leaders who practice empathy are often viewed as more approachable and supportive, which can boost employee morale and productivity. Team members who practice empathy with one another tend to collaborate more effectively and resolve conflicts with greater ease.

In personal relationships, empathy is essential for building intimacy, resolving conflicts, and maintaining strong connections. It fosters a sense of emotional closeness and support that is vital for the health and longevity of relationships. Empathetic partners are more attuned to each other's needs and can navigate challenges with greater resilience.

In conclusion, practicing empathy in difficult conversations is a transformative skill that can lead to better communication, enhanced understanding, and more positive outcomes. It involves active listening, nonverbal cues, validation of feelings, and withholding judgment. Cultivating empathy requires self-awareness, emotional self-regulation, and a willingness to be vulnerable. The benefits of empathy include improved communication, trust-building, effective conflict resolution, and stronger relationships, both in personal and professional spheres. By embracing empathy as a core skill, individuals can create more meaningful and harmonious interactions, even in the most challenging conversations.

Building rapport and trust

Rapport and trust are foundational elements of successful human interactions, whether in personal relationships, professional settings, or any social context. The ability to establish and nurture rapport and trust is a vital skill that can enhance communication, foster positive relationships, and pave the way for collaboration and cooperation. In this section, we will delve into the importance of building rapport and trust, explore strategies for doing so effectively, and examine the far-reaching benefits of these essential interpersonal skills.

Rapport can be defined as a harmonious and positive connection between individuals. It involves creating a sense of ease, comfort, and mutual understanding in interactions. Building rapport is the initial step in the process of establishing trust, as it lays the foundation for meaningful connections.

Active listening is one of the most important skills in rapport building. This entails giving the speaker your whole attention, expressing a sincere interest in what they have to say, and exhibiting empathy by acknowledging and understanding their point of view. Active listening communicates that you value the other person's thoughts and feelings, creating a strong initial bond.

Empathy is another crucial aspect of rapport-building. Empathy involves not only understanding the other person's feelings but also sharing in those emotions. When individuals feel that someone truly understands and empathizes with them, they are more likely to connect on a deeper level. Empathetic gestures, such as offering comfort or support when needed, can further strengthen the rapport.

In addition to active listening and empathy, mirroring and matching are techniques that can enhance rapport. These involve subtly reflecting the other person's body language, tone of voice, or speech patterns. Mirroring and matching help establish a sense of rapport by creating a feeling of similarity and connection. However, it's essential to use these techniques authentically and without overdoing it, as insincerity can damage trust.

Trust, on the other hand, goes beyond the initial connection of rapport. Trust is the conviction that someone can be relied upon, that their actions and words align with their intentions, and that they have our best interests at heart. Building trust takes time and consistent behavior.

The foundations of trust are openness and honesty. Being truthful and forthright in your interactions is essential for building and maintaining trust. When people perceive that you are honest and transparent, they are more likely to trust your intentions and rely on your word.

Reliability is another critical component of trust.

Consistently following through on commitments, meeting deadlines, and keeping promises is vital for establishing trustworthiness. Reliability communicates that you can be counted on to deliver as expected.

Competence also plays a role in trust-building. Demonstrating competence in your area of expertise or responsibility instills confidence in others. When people believe that you are knowledgeable and capable, they are more likely to trust your judgment and decisions.

Consistency in behavior and values is essential for building and maintaining trust. Consistency means that your actions and values align over time, creating a sense of predictability and dependability. When individuals can rely on your consistency, they are more likely to trust your character and intentions.

Openness to feedback and willingness to admit mistakes are indicators of trustworthiness. When you are open to receiving constructive feedback and are willing to acknowledge and rectify your errors, you demonstrate humility and a commitment to growth. People are more likely to trust those who take responsibility for their actions and seek opportunities for improvement.

Developing rapport and trust is important in professional settings just as it is in personal ones. Trust is the cornerstone of productive teamwork, collaboration, and leadership in the workplace. Leaders who cultivate trust within their team members frequently have greater success inspiring and motivating their staff.

Effective communication is a key strategy for building rapport and trust in professional settings. Clear and open communication fosters understanding and reduces misunderstandings and conflicts. Leaders who communicate openly as well as honestly with their teams will likely gain their trust and loyalty.

In team dynamics, trust creates a cohesive and harmonious work environment. Team members who trust one another are more likely to collaborate effectively, share information, and support each other. Trust also enables constructive feedback and healthy debate, leading to better decision-making and problem-solving. Trust is especially critical in client relationships and customer service. Companies that prioritize trustworthiness are more likely to retain loyal customers and establish a positive reputation. Trust is not only earned through the quality of products or services but also through transparent communication, responsiveness to customer concerns, and a commitment to delivering value.

In leadership, building trust is essential for fostering employee engagement and commitment. Members of a trustworthy team feel more confident and devoted to their leader, which boosts productivity and job satisfaction. Trust also plays a role in employee retention, as individuals will likely remain with organizations where they feel valued and trusted.

Trust is a vital component of negotiation and conflict resolution. When parties trust one another, they are more likely to engage in productive discussions and reach mutually beneficial agreements. Trust creates an environment where individuals are willing to compromise and seek win-win solutions.

In conclusion, building rapport and trust are fundamental skills that contribute to positive and meaningful relationships in both personal and professional life. Rapport involves creating a connection through active listening, empathy, and authentic communication. Trust, on the other hand, is earned through honesty, reliability, competence, consistency, and openness to feedback.

The benefits of building rapport and trust are extensive and include improved communication, strengthened relationships, enhanced teamwork, more effective leadership, customer loyalty, and successful negotiation. Whether in personal interactions or professional endeavors, the ability to establish and nurture rapport and trust is a useful asset that can lead to more fulfilling and successful interactions and outcomes. By prioritizing these essential interpersonal skills, individuals and organizations can develop a more harmonious and productive environment for growth and collaboration.

CHAPTER VII

Managing Your Own Emotions

Coping with stress and frustration

Stress and frustration are common experiences in our fast-paced, demanding lives. From the workplace to personal relationships, we encounter situations that challenge our ability to maintain emotional balance. Coping with stress and frustration is essential for our mental and physical well-being. This section will explore the causes of stress and frustration, their impact on our lives, and effective strategies to manage and alleviate these emotions.

Stress often arises when we perceive a situation as demanding or threatening, triggering our body's fight-or-flight response. This physiological reaction is a survival mechanism, but it can lead to chronic stress in modern life if not managed effectively. Common sources of stress involve work-related pressures, financial concerns, family dynamics, health issues, and external events like traffic jams or unexpected delays.

Frustration, on the other hand, typically stems from unmet expectations or obstacles that hinder our progress. It arises when we feel blocked or unable to achieve our goals. Frustration can manifest in various areas of life, such as work, relationships, personal projects, or when dealing with technology and other external challenges.

The impact of stress and frustration on our lives can be profound. Chronic stress can cause an array of physical health problems, such as heart problems, weakened immune systems, and mental health conditions like depression and anxiety. If not managed, frustration can lead to increased irritability, decreased motivation, and a negative impact on our self-esteem and self-worth.

One of the essential strategies for coping with stress and frustration is developing emotional intelligence. Emotional intelligence involves recognizing, understanding, and managing our own emotions and those of others. By honing this skill, we can navigate stressful and frustrating situations more effectively.

Self-awareness is the first stage in developing emotional intelligence. It involves recognizing and acknowledging our emotions without judgment. When we become aware of our stress or frustration, we can take steps to address them. For example, acknowledging it can prompt you to take a short break or exercise deep breathing to calm yourself if you're feeling stressed at work.

Emotional self-regulation is another essential component of emotional intelligence. It involves managing our emotional responses healthily. When stressed or frustrated, practice relaxation techniques including mindfulness meditation, improving muscle relaxation, or deep breathing exercises. These techniques can help lower your heart rate and reduce the physical symptoms of stress.

Empathy is a valuable skill in coping with stress and frustration. By understanding the perspectives and emotions of others, we can develop more patience and tolerance. Empathy can also help us communicate more effectively, especially in situations where frustration arises due to miscommunication or conflicting viewpoints.

Effective communication is crucial in managing stress and frustration, particularly in relationships. Clearly and assertively expressing your thoughts and feelings can prevent misunderstandings and conflicts. At the same time, practice active listening to understand the concerns and perspectives of others fully.

Time management and organization skills can reduce stress by helping you better manage your responsibilities and commitments. Prioritize tasks, set realistic objectives, and break projects into manageable steps. This approach can prevent feeling overwhelmed and reduce frustration caused by perceived time constraints.

To cope with stress, consider adopting a regular exercise routine. Exercise has been demonstrated to lower stress hormones and release endorphins, which are organic mood enhancers. Exercise can be a potent tool for managing stress, whether it's running, yoga, or playing team sports.

Stress and frustration management is greatly aided by having a balanced diet and getting proper nutrients. Steer clear of sugar and caffeine in excess as these can increase stress and cause mood swings. Rather, go for a well-balanced diet full of whole grains, fruits, vegetables, and lean meats. Retaining physical and mental health also requires adequate hydration.

Sleep is essential for emotional stability and stress reduction. Lack of sleep can accelerate stress levels and make it harder for us to handle difficult circumstances. Try to get between seven and nine hours of good sleep every night to help your body and mind cope with stress and annoyance.

Stress can be decreased, and the mind calmed by engaging in relaxation practices like gradual relaxation of muscles, mindfulness, and meditation. These methods encourage relaxation and are especially helpful when dealing with challenging or frustrating circumstances. You can become more adept at maintaining composure and concentration with regular practice.

Getting social support is another effective way to manage stress and annoyance. Speaking with friends, family, or a therapist can help you process your feelings and see your problems from a different angle. Expressing your emotions to people you can trust can help you feel validated and relieved of your emotions.

Taking part in enjoyable hobbies and pursuits can help you detach from tension and annoyance. Engaging in sports, hobbies, or creative endeavors can provide one a sense of happiness and accomplishment, which helps to balance out the bad feelings that come with stress.

Additionally effective strategies for reducing stress and frustration include mindfulness and meditation. By exercising these techniques, you can build a nonjudgmental awareness of your thoughts and feelings as well as present-moment awareness. You can improve your emotional intelligence, lessen your reactivity, and build resilience and serenity by engaging in mindfulness practices.

Furthermore, cognitive-behavioral methods are an effective way to modify thought patterns that lead to frustration and stress. You are able to dispute and challenge unfavorable or unreasonable beliefs that heighten these feelings through cognitive restructuring. You can develop more adaptable and constructive thought patterns as a result of this process.

Seeking professional support from a therapist or a counselor can be beneficial in handling persistent stress or extreme annoyance. These experts can offer you support, direction, and evidence-based coping mechanisms to help you manage challenging emotions. If stress or frustration is severely affecting your mental health and day-to-day functioning, therapy may be especially helpful.

In conclusion, managing stress and frustration is critical to preserving our mental and physical health. Although these feelings are inevitable in life, they can be effectively controlled with the appropriate techniques. Effective strategies for managing stress and frustration include cultivating emotional intelligence, engaging in relaxation exercises, upholding a healthy lifestyle, reaching out to others for support, and, when necessary, seeking professional assistance. People can lessen the negative effects of these emotions and enhance their general quality of life by putting these strategies into practice.

Self-regulation techniques

Self-regulation, often called self-control or emotional regulation, is a fundamental skill that allow individuals to manage their thoughts, emotions, and behaviors effectively. It is crucial in various aspects of life, including personal relationships, decision-making, and overall well-being. Self-regulation techniques are tools and strategies that help individuals develop and maintain control over their impulses and emotional reactions. This section will explore the importance of self-regulation, different self-regulation techniques, and their practical applications in daily life.

Self-regulation is a multifaceted skill encompassing several dimensions, including emotional, impulse, and cognitive regulation. Emotional regulation involves recognizing and managing one's emotions, such as anger, anxiety, or sadness, in a healthy and adaptive manner. Impulse control is the capacity to resist immediate temptations or urges in favor of long-term goals and values. Cognitive regulation involves managing one's thoughts and cognitive processes, such as attention, focus, and problem-solving.

The importance of self-regulation cannot be overstated. It underlies many critical life skills and contributes to personal and professional success. In personal relationships, self-regulation helps individuals navigate conflicts, communicate effectively, and maintain healthy boundaries. In the workplace, it plays a role in decision-making, stress management, and teamwork. Additionally, self-regulation is closely linked to mental health and overall well-being, as it reduces the risk of impulsivity- driven behaviors and emotional distress.

One of the key self-regulation techniques is mindfulness meditation. Mindfulness entails paying deliberate attention to the present moment without judgment. Through regular mindfulness practice, individuals can become more conscious of their thoughts and feelings as well as learn to respond to them in a non-reactive and balanced way. Mindfulness meditation can help reduce stress, increase emotional regulation, and improve overall well-being.

Breathing exercises are another effective self-regulation technique. Deep breathing techniques, like diaphragmatic breathing or the 4-7-8 technique, can help individuals calm their nervous system, reduce anxiety, and regain emotional control. These strategies are simple to practice and can be used in various situations, from managing workplace stress to handling intense emotions in personal relationships.

Cognitive reappraisal is a self-regulation technique that involves reframing one's thoughts and changing the way a situation is perceived. By challenging and modifying negative or irrational thought patterns, individuals can reduce emotional distress and make more balanced decisions. Cognitive reappraisal is often used in cognitive-behavioral therapy (CBT) and can be a valuable tool for managing stress and anxiety.

Physical activity is another powerful self-regulation technique. It has been shown that exercise lowers stress, elevates mood, and strengthens emotional control.

Regular physical activity can raise the production of endorphins, which are naturally occurring mood enhancers. This can be achieved through strength training, yoga, or aerobic exercises. Another healthy way to release stress and pent-up emotions is through exercise.

A method called progressive muscle relaxation entails methodically tensing and then relaxing various body muscle groups. Through this process, people can learn to recognize and release physical tension. When it comes to easing the physical signs of stress, like headaches and tense muscles, progressive muscle relaxation can be very helpful. It can be used as a stand-alone method or in combination with other relaxation exercises.

Time management and organization skills contribute to self-regulation by helping individuals prioritize tasks and responsibilities. Effective time management prevents procrastination and reduces the stress caused by missed deadlines or rushed work. Techniques such as creating to-do lists, setting goals, and using time management tools can improve productivity and reduce the likelihood of impulsive decisions.

Self-reflection is an essential self-regulation technique. It involves taking time to examine one's thoughts, emotions, and behaviors. Self-reflection allows individuals to identify patterns of behavior, triggers for emotional reactions, and areas where self-regulation may be needed. Journaling or keeping a diary can be a valuable self-reflection tool, as it provides a record of thoughts and emotions over time.

Another effective self-regulation technique is the practice of setting and maintaining personal boundaries. Healthy boundaries help individuals protect their emotional and mental well-being by defining limits in various relationships and situations. Establishing clear boundaries communicates self-respect and allows individuals to assertively communicate their needs and expectations. Boundaries are crucial for keeping healthy relationships and reducing the risk of emotional manipulation or burnout.

In practical terms, self-regulation techniques can be applied to numerous aspects of daily life. In the workplace, individuals can use mindfulness techniques to reduce stress, cognitive reappraisal to manage challenging situations, and time management skills to prioritize tasks effectively. In personal relationships, self-regulation techniques can help individuals communicate more calmly and assertively, manage conflicts, and set boundaries to protect their emotional well-being.

For students, self-regulation techniques can be valuable in managing academic stress, improving concentration, and enhancing study habits. Techniques like time management and goal-setting can help students stay organized and achieve their academic goals. Mindfulness practices can reduce test anxiety and improve focus during study sessions.

In conclusion, self-regulation techniques are essential tools for managing thoughts, emotions, and behaviors effectively. These techniques encompass various dimensions of self-regulation, including emotional regulation, impulse control, and cognitive regulation. Developing self-regulation skills can lead to improved personal relationships, enhanced decision-making, and better mental health. By incorporating self-regulation techniques into daily life, individuals can navigate stress, make more balanced choices, and ultimately lead happier and more fulfilling lives.

Maintaining composure during tough conversations

Tough conversations are a part of life, whether they occur in personal relationships, professional settings, or other social contexts. These discussions often involve sensitive topics, disagreements, or emotionally charged situations, making it challenging to maintain composure and effectively communicate. However, the ability to stay composed during tough conversations is a valuable skill that can lead to better outcomes, improved relationships, and reduced stress. In this section, we will explore the importance of maintaining composure during tough conversations, strategies for doing so, and the benefits of mastering this skill.

The significance of maintaining composure during tough conversations cannot be overstated. How we handle such discussions can have a deep effect on the quality of our relationships and the resolutions of conflicts. When individuals remain composed, they create an environment that encourages open and honest communication, reduces defensiveness, and fosters understanding. Composure enables us to think more clearly, listen attentively, and respond empathetically, leading to more productive and constructive conversations.

One of the first strategies for maintaining composure during tough conversations is practicing active listening. Active listening entails offering your full attention to the speaker, without interrupting or formulating your response while they are talking. It demands patience and a willingness to understand the speaker's point of view, even if you may not agree with it. By actively listening, you signal to the other person that their perspective is valued and respected, which can de-escalate tensions and promote a more composed atmosphere.

Empathy is another crucial aspect of maintaining composure. Empathy includes not only understanding but also sharing in the feelings of others. When individuals practice empathy during tough conversations, they can better connect with the emotions and experiences of the other person. This shared emotional understanding can lead to more compassionate and composed responses. Empathetic gestures, such as offering comfort or support when needed, can further enhance composure.

Maintaining composure also requires emotional self-regulation. Emotional self-regulation involves managing our emotional responses effectively, particularly in challenging situations. When faced with tough conversations, individuals should practice techniques like deep breathing, mindfulness, or relaxation exercises to remain calm and composed. These techniques help reduce the physiological effects of stress and anxiety, such as increased heart rate or shallow breathing.

Maintaining a non-reactive and non-defensive stance is crucial in tough conversations. It's common for emotions to run high, and individuals may feel attacked or criticized. However, answering defensively can escalate the situation and hinder productive communication. Instead, strive to remain calm and composed, even in the face of criticism or hostility. A composed response can help defuse tension and create an environment where more rational and empathetic dialogue can occur.

Another effective strategy is to take a break when needed. If a tough conversation becomes too emotionally charged or overwhelming, it's acceptable to request a brief break to regain composure. During this break, engage in calming activities such as deep breathing, a short walk, or mindfulness exercises. Taking a step back allows you to manage your emotions and return to the conversation with a clearer mind.

Staying focused on the issue at hand and avoiding personal attacks is essential for maintaining composure. In tough conversations, it's easy to become sidetracked by unrelated issues or to resort to blaming and criticizing the other person. Instead, remain focused on the specific problem or topic that needs to be addressed. Use the "I" statements to express your feelings and concerns without assigning blame.

Choosing the right time and place for tough conversations can contribute to maintaining composure. Timing matters, and it's essential to consider the other person's emotional state and availability. Opt for a private and quiet setting where both parties can concentrate on the conversation without distractions. Avoid having tough conversations when either party is exhausted or highly stressed, as it can hinder composure and effective communication.

Practice self-awareness throughout tough conversations. Reflect on your own emotions and reactions, and recognize your triggers and biases. Being self-aware can help you stay composed by preventing impulsive responses driven by anger or defensiveness. It allows you to make more conscious choices in how you react to the situation.

Managing expectations is another key strategy for maintaining composure. Recognize that tough conversations may not always lead to immediate resolution or agreement. Sometimes, the goal of such discussions is simply to express feelings, gain understanding, or establish boundaries. Having realistic expectations can reduce frustration and disappointment, allowing you to stay composed and concentrated on the process rather than the outcome.

The benefits of maintaining composure during tough conversations are manifold. Firstly, it facilitates more effective communication. When individuals remain composed, they are better able to express their thoughts and feelings precisely, without becoming overwhelmed by emotion. This clarity can lead to a better comprehension of each other's perspectives and the underlying issues at hand.

Composure also fosters empathy and understanding. When people perceive that you are composed and attentive, they are more likely to feel heard and valued. This, in turn, can encourage them to share their thoughts and feelings more openly. Empathy and understanding contribute to a more positive and empathetic conversation.

Moreover, maintaining composure can help de-escalate conflicts and reduce defensiveness. In tough conversations, conflicts often arise due to misunderstandings or differing viewpoints. A composed demeanor can create an emotionally safe environment where both parties feel respected and heard. This reduces the risk of confrontations and allows for more constructive dialogue.

In personal relationships, maintaining composure is crucial for building trust and maintaining strong connections. When individuals can communicate calmly and empathetically during tough conversations, they demonstrate respect and emotional intelligence. This, in turn, contributes to healthier and more resilient relationships.

In professional settings, composure is particularly valuable. It enhances leadership skills, conflict resolution abilities, and teamwork. Leaders who maintain composure are often viewed as role models who can inspire and motivate their teams. Effective communication and composure are also key to resolving workplace conflicts and fostering a harmonious work environment.

In conclusion, maintaining composure during tough conversations is a vital skill that can result in better communication, enhanced relationships, and reduced stress. Strategies for maintaining composure include active listening, empathy, emotional self-regulation, non-reactivity, taking breaks when necessary, staying focused on the issue, choosing the right time and place, practicing self-awareness, and managing expectations. The benefits of composure are numerous, from more effective communication and conflict resolution to the strengthening of personal and professional relationships. By honing this skill, individuals can navigate tough conversations with grace and empathy, ultimately leading to more positive outcomes and healthier connections.

CHAPTER VIII

Conflict Resolution Techniques

Mediation and negotiation strategies

Conflict is an inevitable part of human interaction, arising in various contexts, from personal relationships to the workplace. Resolving conflicts efficiently is crucial for maintaining healthy relationships, fostering collaboration, and achieving positive outcomes. Mediation and negotiation are two powerful conflict resolution techniques that provide structured approaches to address disputes and reach mutually agreeable solutions. In this section, we will delve into the concepts of mediation and negotiation, explore their key strategies, and examine their applications in different settings.

Mediation is a voluntary and facilitated process in which a neutral third party, or the mediator, assists disputing parties in resolving their conflict. The mediator's role is to facilitate communication, guide the parties in identifying their interests and requirements, and help them generate mutually acceptable solutions. Unlike arbitration, where a third party makes a binding decision, mediation empowers the parties to reach a resolution themselves, making it a collaborative and consensual process.

One of the central strategies in mediation is open communication. The mediator creates a secure and structured environment where the parties can express their concerns, feelings, and perspectives without a fear of judgment or retaliation. Effective communication allows the parties to gain a better understanding of each other's viewpoints, which is essential for finding common ground and building trust.

Active listening is another critical element of mediation. The mediator listens attentively to each party, demonstrating empathy and understanding. Additionally, the mediator encourages the disputing parties to listen actively to each other. Active listening fosters a sense of being heard and valued, which can de-escalate tensions and facilitate cooperation.

The mediator uses various questioning techniques to guide the conversation and help the parties explore their interests and underlying needs. Open-ended questions encourage the parties to elaborate on their thoughts and feelings, while clarifying questions ensure a shared understanding of the issues. Reflective questions can help the parties gain insight into their own positions and those of the other party.

During mediation, the mediator may employ reframing as a strategy to rephrase or reframe statements made by the parties. Reframing can help change the perspective on an issue, making it easier for the parties to consider alternative solutions. For example, if one party says, "I need this promotion because I've been here the longest," the mediator might reframe it as, "It sounds like you value seniority and experience in your role."

Another key strategy in mediation is brainstorming. Once the parties have identified their interests and needs, they can work together to generate a variety of potential solutions. Brainstorming encourages creativity and flexibility, as it allows for the exploration of innovative options that may not have been initially apparent. The mediator facilitates the brainstorming process, ensuring that all ideas are considered and that no one dominates the discussion.

Once potential solutions have been identified, the mediator helps the parties evaluate and assess them. This involves discussing the advantages and disadvantages of each option and considering their feasibility and impact. The goal is to arrive at a solution that addresses the parties' interests and needs while maintaining the principles of fairness and mutual respect.

Negotiation, on the other hand, is a broader conflict resolution process that encompasses a wide range of strategies and tactics to reach agreements between parties with differing interests or positions. Negotiations can occur in various settings, including business transactions, labor disputes, international diplomacy, and personal relationships. Negotiators aim to find mutually acceptable compromises and trade-offs that balance the interests and needs of both sides.

A fundamental strategy in negotiation is preparation. Successful negotiators invest time in researching and understanding the issues at hand, the interests and positions of the parties involved, and the potential alternatives to a negotiated agreement. Being well-prepared gives negotiators a strategic advantage, allowing them to make educated decisions and respond effectively during negotiations.

Effective communication is at the heart of negotiation strategies. Negotiators must be skilled in both speaking and listening. Articulating their positions clearly and persuasively is essential, as is actively listening to the other party to understand their concerns and perspectives. Good communication skills enable negotiators to build rapport, establish trust, and create an open and constructive dialogue.

Interest-based negotiation, often referred to as principled negotiation, focuses on the parties' underlying interests and needs rather than their fixed positions. Negotiators using this strategy seek to identify common ground and mutually beneficial solutions by exploring the interests that motivate each party's position. Interest-based negotiation encourages problem-solving and collaboration rather than adversarial competition.

Another negotiation strategy is the use of concession and compromise. Concession involves making concessions or giving up something of value to the other party in exchange for something in return. Compromise involves finding a middle ground that partially satisfies both parties' interests. Effective negotiators strike a balance between assertiveness (advocating for their own interests) and cooperativeness (seeking mutually acceptable solutions).

The negotiation process often involves exploring alternatives and BATNAs (Best Alternative to a Negotiated Agreement). A BATNA is the course of action a party will take if negotiations fail to achieve a satisfactory agreement. Understanding their BATNA empowers negotiators to assess the value of a proposed agreement and make strategic decisions during negotiations.

Negotiators also use various persuasion and influence tactics to move the other party toward agreement. These tactics may include appealing to the other party's interests, using logic and reasoning, framing the issues in a favorable light, and building trust and rapport. Negotiators must use persuasion ethically and avoid manipulative or coercive tactics.

Negotiation strategies can vary based on the nature of the conflict and the relationship between the parties. For example, in distributive negotiations, where there is a fixed amount of resources to be divided, negotiators often engage in competitive strategies to claim a larger share. In contrast, integrative negotiations involve creating value and expanding the available resources through cooperation and creative problem-solving.

The benefits of mediation and negotiation strategies are extensive. In mediation, parties keep control over the outcome and actively participate in shaping the resolution. This can lead to more durable and satisfying agreements, as the parties are more likely to comply voluntarily. Mediation also tends to be less adversarial and confrontational, preserving relationships and reducing the emotional toll of conflicts.

Negotiation, too, offers numerous advantages. It allows parties to reach agreements that balance their interests and needs, often resulting in win-win outcomes. Negotiation is a versatile process that can be adapted to various situations and conflicts, from business deals to marital disputes. It is a valuable skill in both personal and professional life, enabling individuals to advocate for their interests while maintaining constructive relationships.

In conclusion, mediation and negotiation are two powerful conflict resolution techniques that offer structured approaches to resolving disputes and reaching mutually agreeable solutions. Mediation involves the guidance of a neutral third party, the mediator, who facilitates communication, guides the parties in exploring their interests, and helps generate solutions. Negotiation, on the other hand, is a broader process that encompasses various strategies and tactics to reach agreements between parties with differing interests. Both mediation and negotiation emphasize effective communication, understanding interests, and exploring creative solutions. These techniques are valuable tools for addressing conflicts and achieving positive outcomes in a wide range of settings, ultimately promoting cooperation, collaboration, and healthier relationships.

Win-win solutions

Conflict is a natural part of human interaction, arising in various facets of life, from personal relationships to professional settings. Effective conflict resolution techniques are essential for addressing disputes and reaching mutually beneficial solutions. One such technique is the pursuit of win-win solutions, a concept rooted in the belief that conflicts can be addressed in a way that satisfies the interests and requirements of all parties involved. In this section, we will explore the principles of win-win solutions, delve into strategies for achieving them, and examine the benefits they offer in different contexts.

Win-win solutions, also known as integrative or collaborative solutions, represent a departure from the traditional win-lose paradigm where one party's gain comes at the expense of the other. In win-win approaches, the goal is to find solutions that not only resolve the immediate conflict but also create value and benefit all parties involved. This approach recognizes that conflicts often arise from differing interests and needs, and the challenge is to identify common ground and creative solutions that address these diverse concerns.

One of the central principles of win-win solutions is interest-based negotiation. Rather than focusing on fixed positions, interest-based negotiation seeks to understand the underlying interests and needs that drive each party's position. By exploring these interests, negotiators can often uncover shared goals and priorities, paving the way for collaborative problem-solving. Interest-based negotiation encourages parties to move beyond adversarial tactics and competition and instead foster cooperation and mutual gain.

Effective communication is pivotal in achieving win-win solutions. Parties engaged in a conflict must be willing to participate in open and honest dialogue, sharing their concerns, perspectives, and needs. Listening attentively to the other party's viewpoint is equally important. Active listening helps build rapport and trust, fosters empathy, and creates an atmosphere conducive to finding common ground.

Transparency and information sharing are integral components of win-win solutions. Parties should be willing to provide relevant information and data to support their positions and engage in a process of full disclosure. Transparency helps build trust and credibility, reducing the likelihood of hidden agendas or manipulation. When all parties have access to the same information, they can make informed decisions and explore mutually beneficial options.

Brainstorming is a valuable strategy for generating win-win solutions. During the brainstorming process, parties work together to generate a wide range of possible solutions, even those that may seem unconventional or innovative. The goal is to promote creativity and flexibility in problem-solving. Brainstorming allows parties to explore possibilities they may not have considered initially, expanding the scope of potential win-win outcomes.

Trade-offs and concessions are essential elements of win-win solutions. Parties may need to make concessions by giving up something of value to meet the interests and needs of the other party. Effective negotiation involves a willingness to compromise, recognizing that it may be necessary to achieve a mutually satisfying agreement. By making trade-offs, parties can create a balance that meets their core concerns while accommodating the concerns of others.

A focus on the long-term relationship is a hallmark of win-win solutions. Parties recognize that the resolution of the current conflict should not come at the expense of damaging the ongoing relationship. This perspective is particularly important in contexts where parties are likely to interact in the future, such as workplace relationships or ongoing business partnerships. Prioritizing the preservation of the relationship encourages parties to seek solutions that are not only fair but also sustainable.

Win-win solutions often involve collaborative problem-solving and negotiation techniques, such as identifying areas of shared interest, exploring options for mutual gain, and considering the long-term implications of the agreement. Parties should be willing to engage in principled negotiation, which means focusing on the merits of the issues at hand rather than resorting to manipulation or positional bargaining.

Win-win solutions offer numerous advantages across various contexts. In personal relationships, they promote understanding and empathy, strengthen trust and intimacy, and create an atmosphere of cooperation. By seeking win-win solutions, individuals can address conflicts without harming the quality of their relationships, fostering healthier and more resilient bonds.

In the workplace, win-win solutions enhance teamwork, collaboration, and employee morale. They empower employees to engage in problem-solving and contribute to decision-making, which can lead to a more positive and inclusive work environment. Win-win solutions also reduce the risk of escalated conflicts, grievances, and turnover, contributing to higher job satisfaction and retention rates.

In business negotiations, win-win solutions can lead to more profitable and sustainable agreements. They enable parties to explore opportunities for mutual value creation, identify innovative solutions, and build long-term partnerships. Companies that prioritize win-win negotiations tend to have better relationships with suppliers, clients, and other stakeholders, ultimately enhancing their competitive advantage.

Win-win solutions are also valuable in international diplomacy and conflict resolution. They encourage nations to seek peaceful and collaborative resolutions to disputes, reducing the risk of armed conflicts and promoting global stability. By finding mutually beneficial solutions, countries can work together to address complex challenges, such as trade agreements, environmental issues, or regional conflicts.

Moreover, win-win solutions contribute to individual well-being by reducing stress and promoting a sense of empowerment and control over one's circumstances. When individuals engage in constructive problem-solving and find resolutions that satisfy their interests, they experience a greater sense of fulfillment and accomplishment. This, in turn, supports mental and emotional well-being.

However, it is important to acknowledge that achieving win-win solutions is not always possible or appropriate in every situation. Some conflicts may involve irreconcilable differences, power imbalances, or ethical considerations that make mutually beneficial solutions challenging to attain. In such cases, alternative conflict resolution techniques, such as compromise or arbitration, may be more suitable.

In conclusion, win-win solutions represent a proactive and collaborative approach to conflict resolution, aiming to solve disputes in ways that fulfill the interests and needs of all parties involved. Key principles of win-win solutions include interest-based negotiation, effective communication, transparency, brainstorming, trade-offs, and a focus on the long-term relationship. These principles can be employed in different contexts, from personal relationships to the workplace and international diplomacy. By prioritizing win-win solutions, individuals and organizations can foster cooperation, enhance relationships, and achieve more positive outcomes while maintaining the quality of their interactions.

Dealing with toxic individuals

In the intricate web of human relationships, we inevitably encounter a diverse array of individuals. While most interactions are positive and enriching, some can become challenging, especially when dealing with toxic individuals. Toxic individuals are those whose behavior, attitudes, and actions consistently have a negative impact on others, often causing conflict, stress, and emotional turmoil. Successfully navigating these relationships requires a skill set that combines conflict resolution techniques with emotional intelligence and self-care. In this section, we will explore the concept of toxic individuals, delve into strategies for dealing with them, and examine the importance of self-preservation in such encounters.

Identifying toxic individuals is the first step in addressing the challenges they present. Toxicity can manifest in various ways, including chronic negativity, manipulative behavior, constant criticism, excessive control, and a tendency to create drama or chaos. Toxic individuals often drain the energy and emotional well-being of those around them, leaving a trail of turmoil in their wake. Recognizing these patterns is essential for initiating the process of dealing with such individuals effectively.

Setting boundaries is a fundamental strategy when dealing with toxic individuals. Establishing clear and healthy boundaries is vital for protecting your emotional and mental well-being. Boundaries define what behaviors, actions, or comments you find acceptable or unacceptable in a relationship. Communicate these boundaries assertively but respectfully, and be prepared to enforce them if necessary. Boundaries act as a protective barrier against the toxicity of others, preserving your self-esteem and emotional equilibrium.

Practicing assertiveness is another critical technique for addressing toxic individuals. Assertiveness involves expressing your thoughts, feelings, and needs in a direct and respectful manner. When confronted with toxic behavior, assertiveness allows you to communicate your boundaries and concerns clearly. It also prevents you from becoming passive or aggressive in your responses. Assertive communication conveys your self-respect and can discourage toxic individuals from crossing your boundaries.

Active listening plays an essential role in managing interactions with toxic individuals. By actively listening, you demonstrate empathy and a willingness to understand their perspective. This can de-escalate tense situations and encourage the toxic individual to feel heard and valued. While it may not change their behavior, active listening can create a more constructive atmosphere for communication.

Maintaining emotional detachment is a strategy that prevents toxic individuals from triggering emotional reactions. Toxic individuals often seek to provoke emotional responses in others, whether through criticism, manipulation, or dramatic outbursts. By remaining emotionally detached, you protect yourself from being drawn into their negative dynamics. Emotional detachment allows you to respond calmly and rationally, reducing the power that toxic individuals have over your emotions.

Limiting contact with toxic individuals is sometimes necessary for self-preservation. While it may not always be possible to completely sever ties, reducing the frequency and depth of interaction can significantly reduce the impact of their toxicity. This can be particularly important if the toxic individual is a family member or coworker with whom you must maintain some level of connection. Limiting contact allows you to create emotional distance and minimize exposure to their harmful behaviors.

Practicing self-care is a crucial aspect of dealing with toxic individuals. The stress and emotional toll of such relationships can be significant. Engaging in self-care activities, such as mindfulness, exercise, relaxation techniques, and asking support from friends or a therapist, can help mitigate the negative effects of the relationship. Self-care is essential for replenishing your emotional reserves and maintaining your mental well-being.

Detaching from the need for approval or validation from toxic individuals is another key strategy. Toxic individuals often wield their approval or disapproval as a form of control. By recognizing your own worth and seeking validation from within, you become less susceptible to their manipulations. Detaching from their opinions and judgments empowers you to make decisions that prioritize your well-being and values.

Maintaining perspective is important when dealing with toxic individuals. Remember that their behavior is a reflection of their issues, insecurities, and unresolved conflicts, rather than a judgment of your worth. By reframing their actions as a reflection of their internal struggles, you can avoid taking their behavior personally and maintain a sense of self-worth.

Seeking support from a therapist or a counselor can be invaluable when dealing with toxic individuals. These professionals can provide guidance, validation, and coping strategies tailored to your specific situation. Therapy can also help you process your emotions and develop resilience in the face of ongoing toxicity.

In some cases, disengagement and distancing may be the only viable option for dealing with toxic individuals. This decision should be made after careful consideration of the relationship's impact on your well-being. Disengagement can involve cutting ties, distancing yourself emotionally, or even seeking legal protection, depending on the severity of the situation. Prioritizing your security and well-being is paramount when dealing with extreme toxicity.

It is important to acknowledge that dealing with toxic individuals can be emotionally draining as well as challenging. Toxic individuals often resist change and may not be receptive to attempts at resolution or improvement. In such cases, your well-being and emotional health must take precedence. You have the right to protect yourself from harm and make choices that prioritize your own happiness and peace of mind.

In conclusion, dealing with toxic individuals requires a combination of conflict resolution techniques, emotional intelligence, and self-care strategies. Identifying toxic behavior, setting boundaries, practicing assertiveness, active listening, emotional detachment, limiting contact, self-care, detaching from the need for approval, maintaining perspective, seeking support, and, when necessary, disengaging from the relationship are all valuable strategies for navigating these challenging interactions. Remember that your well-being is paramount, and you have the right to protect yourself from the harmful effects of toxicity. By carrying out these strategies, you can lessen the impact of toxic individuals on your life and maintain your emotional equilibrium.

CHAPTER IX

Navigating Difficult Conversations at Work

Handling difficult colleagues and superiors

Navigating workplace dynamics can be a complex endeavor, as it often involves interactions with colleagues and superiors of varying personalities and temperaments. While many workplace relationships are characterized by cooperation and support, there may be instances where you encounter difficult colleagues or superiors. Dealing with such individuals effectively is a skill that not only contributes to your professional growth but also fosters a healthier work environment. In this section, we will explore the challenges posed by difficult colleagues and superiors, discuss strategies for handling them, and underscore the importance of maintaining professionalism and self-care in these interactions.

Difficult colleagues and superiors come in various forms, each presenting unique challenges. Some colleagues may exhibit behaviors such as chronic negativity, passive-aggressiveness, or an inability to collaborate effectively, making it challenging to work with them as part of a team. Superiors, on the other hand, may display traits like micromanagement, favoritism, or a lack of communication skills, which can create tension and hinder your professional growth. Recognizing these behaviors is the first stage in addressing the challenges they pose. When dealing with difficult colleagues and superiors, it is essential to approach the situation with professionalism and empathy. Maintaining a respectful and considerate demeanor is crucial, as it sets the tone for the interaction and demonstrates your commitment to resolving the issue amicably. Avoid reacting emotionally or defensively, as this can escalate the conflict and undermine your credibility. Instead, focus on fostering a constructive and open dialogue.

Effective communication is a cornerstone of managing relationships with difficult colleagues and superiors. When issues arise, initiate a conversation in a non-confrontational manner, expressing your concerns and seeking to understand their perspective. Actively listen to their responses and avoid interrupting or making assumptions. By demonstrating your willingness to engage in a productive dialogue, you create an opportunity for mutual understanding and conflict resolution.

Assertiveness is a valuable skill when addressing difficult colleagues and superiors. Assertive communication involves expressing your thoughts, feelings, and needs in a direct and respectful manner. Clearly communicate your boundaries and expectations, ensuring that your voice is heard and your concerns are acknowledged. Avoid being passive or overly aggressive, as these communication styles can hinder the resolution of conflicts.

Seeking common ground and collaboration is essential in managing difficult workplace relationships. Identify shared goals or interests with your colleagues and superiors and emphasize the benefits of working together towards these objectives. Collaborative efforts can build rapport and create a sense of partnership, making it easier to address and resolve conflicts.

When faced with difficult colleagues, consider leveraging the support of your team or supervisor. Discuss the issue with trusted colleagues who may have experienced similar challenges or can provide valuable insights.

Collaborating with your team to address the issue collectively can also lead to more effective solutions. Additionally, involve your supervisor or manager if necessary, providing them with context and seeking their guidance in finding a resolution.

For interactions with difficult superiors, it may be beneficial to engage in a reflective and solution-oriented conversation. Express your desire to work together effectively and seek their opinions on ways to enhance the working relationship. Frame the conversation as a possibility for growth and development, demonstrating your commitment to your professional success.

In cases where your attempts at communication and collaboration prove unsuccessful, it may be necessary to escalate the issue through formal channels. Many organizations have mechanisms in place for addressing workplace conflicts, such as HR departments or grievance procedures. Utilize these resources to ensure that your concerns are addressed and that the appropriate steps are taken to resolve the issue.

While addressing difficult colleagues and superiors is essential for maintaining a healthy work environment, it is equally important to prioritize self-care. The emotional toll of navigating challenging workplace relationships can be significant, leading to stress, burnout, and reduced job satisfaction. Engaging in self-care activities, like mindfulness, exercise, and asking support from friends or a therapist, can help mitigate the adverse effects of these interactions and protect your emotional well-being.

Maintaining perspective is critical when dealing with difficult colleagues and superiors. Recognize that their behavior may be driven by their own insecurities, pressures, or challenges, rather than a reflection of your worth or abilities. By reframing their actions as a manifestation of their internal struggles, you can avoid taking their behavior personally and maintain your self-esteem.

Flexibility and adaptability are critical when working with different personalities and communication styles. Recognize that individuals may have diverse ways of approaching tasks and challenges, and be open to adapting your own communication and work style to accommodate these differences. Flexibility can foster a more harmonious working relationship and reduce the likelihood of conflict.

Building a support network within and outside of the workplace can be invaluable in dealing with difficult colleagues and superiors. Trusted colleagues, mentors, or friends can provide guidance, perspective, and emotional support. Sharing your experiences and asking advice from others who have faced same challenges can help you navigate difficult situations more effectively.

It is important to remember that you have control over your own reactions and behaviors in workplace interactions. While you may not be able to change the behavior of difficult colleagues or superiors, you can choose how you respond to their actions. Maintaining professionalism, self-care, and effective communication strategies are within your power and can significantly influence the outcomes of these interactions.

In conclusion, dealing with difficult colleagues and superiors is an integral part of navigating workplace dynamics. Recognizing and addressing challenging behaviors with professionalism and empathy is essential for maintaining a healthy work environment and fostering your own professional growth. Effective communication, assertiveness, collaboration, and self-care are key strategies for managing workplace relationships successfully. By prioritizing these strategies and maintaining a positive perspective, you can navigate difficult workplace interactions with resilience and professionalism.

Workplace conflict resolution

Conflict is an inherent part of human interaction, and the workplace is no exception. In any organization, individuals with diverse backgrounds, interests, and personalities come together, making conflicts virtually inevitable. However, the key to a healthy and productive work environment lies not in the absence of conflict, but in the organization's ability to manage and resolve it effectively. Workplace conflict resolution is a critical skill that enables individuals and teams to address disputes, foster collaboration, and maintain a positive work atmosphere. In this section, we will explore the dynamics of workplace conflict, delve into strategies for resolution, and emphasize the importance of cultivating a culture that encourages constructive conflict management.

Workplace conflicts can arise from various sources, ranging from differences in communication styles and work methodologies to more complex issues like competition for resources, power struggles, or conflicting values. Conflict can manifest as interpersonal disputes between coworkers, disagreements between employees and supervisors, or even broader organizational conflicts. Regardless of its origins, unresolved conflict can lead to negative consequences, including decreased morale, reduced productivity, and a toxic work environment.

One of the fundamental principles of workplace conflict resolution is transparent and honest communication. Effective communication acts as the foundation for addressing conflicts constructively. When conflicts arise, individuals should be encouraged to express their concerns, perspectives, and feelings without fear of reprisal. Active listening is equally crucial—listening attentively to others fosters empathy and understanding, helping to de-escalate tensions and promote cooperation.

A structured approach to conflict resolution involves identifying the root causes of the conflict. In many cases, conflicts are not just surface-level disagreements but are rooted in underlying issues or unmet needs. By probing deeper, individuals can gain insights into what is driving the conflict and develop more targeted solutions. For example, a conflict between two colleagues over project responsibilities may be linked to a lack of clarity in roles and expectations.

Constructive problem-solving is a key strategy for workplace conflict resolution. Once the underlying causes of a conflict have been identified, individuals and teams can work collaboratively to find solutions that address these root issues. Brainstorming, negotiation, and consensus-building techniques can all play a role in this process. The goal is to identify win-win solutions that fulfill the interests and needs of all parties involved, rather than imposing unilateral decisions that may lead to further conflict.

Setting transparent and healthy boundaries is essential for preventing conflicts from escalating. Boundaries define what behaviors and actions are considered acceptable or unacceptable in the workplace. Communicating these boundaries assertively but respectfully is crucial. It helps establish mutual respect and ensures that individuals understand the expectations regarding behavior and interactions. When boundaries are crossed, addressing the issue promptly and assertively can prevent conflicts from escalating.

In situations where conflicts persist despite attempts at resolution, it may be necessary to involve a neutral third party, such as a mediator or arbitrator. Mediation is a voluntary and facilitated process in which a neutral third party helps in disputing parties in reaching a resolution.

Arbitration, conversely, involves a third party making a binding decision after considering the arguments from both sides. These alternative dispute resolution methods can be valuable in more complex or intractable conflicts.

Conflict resolution is not solely an individual endeavor; organizations are significant in shaping the culture and processes that influence how conflicts are managed. Cultivating a culture of constructive conflict management is essential for addressing workplace conflicts effectively. This includes fostering open communication, promoting active listening, and providing conflict resolution training for employees at all levels. By emphasizing the importance of addressing conflicts promptly and constructively, organizations can create an environment where individuals are empowered to resolve disputes.

Leaders and managers have a particularly influential role in workplace conflict resolution. They should lead by example, demonstrating effective conflict management skills and encouraging open and honest communication among their teams. When conflicts arise, leaders should be accessible and approachable, creating an atmosphere where employees feel comfortable bringing their concerns forward. Additionally, providing leadership development and conflict resolution training can enhance leaders' abilities to manage conflicts within their teams. Transparency in conflict resolution processes is critical for building trust within an organization. Employees should have confidence that their concerns will be taken seriously and addressed fairly. Transparent processes ensure that individuals understand the steps involved in conflict resolution, from reporting the issue to reaching a resolution. Transparency also helps avoid perceptions of bias or favoritism, which can exacerbate conflicts. Monitoring and feedback mechanisms are valuable for assessing the effectiveness of conflict resolution processes and identifying areas for improvement.

Organizations can solicit feedback from employees about their experiences with conflict resolution and use this input to refine their approaches. Regularly reviewing conflict resolution outcomes and analyzing trends can help organizations identify recurring issues and develop targeted interventions.

The benefits of effective workplace conflict resolution are numerous. When conflicts are managed constructively, they can lead to improved problem-solving, increased innovation, and enhanced team dynamics. Conflict resolution also contributes to a more positive and supportive work environment, which can boost employee morale and job satisfaction. Moreover, resolving conflicts promptly prevents them from festering and escalating, reducing the likelihood of costly and protracted disputes.

In conclusion, workplace conflict resolution is a vital skill and organizational practice that promotes a harmonious and productive work environment. Conflicts will inevitably arise, but their resolution can lead to positive outcomes when approached constructively. Open and honest communication, problem-solving, boundary-setting, and a culture of constructive conflict management are key components of effective conflict resolution. Organizations that prioritize these strategies and provide leadership support can create workplaces where conflicts are addressed promptly and professionally, ultimately fostering a healthier and more collaborative work environment.

Strategies for creating a harmonious work environment

A harmonious work environment is one where employees collaborate effectively, communicate openly, and feel a sense of well-being and satisfaction. Such an environment not only enhances productivity but also contributes to the whole success and reputation of an organization. Creating and maintaining a harmonious work environment is a multifaceted endeavor that involves strategies focused on fostering positive relationships, promoting open communication, ensuring fair treatment, and nurturing employee well-being. In this section, we will explore the key strategies for creating a harmonious work environment and highlight their benefits for both individuals and organizations.

One of the fundamental pillars of a harmonious work environment is building positive relationships among colleagues. Positive relationships are characterized by mutual respect, trust, and support. Team-building activities, collaborative projects, and social events can help employees connect on a personal level and develop a sense of camaraderie. When individuals genuinely like and trust their colleagues, they are more likely to work together harmoniously and resolve conflicts constructively.

Open and transparent communication is another cornerstone of a harmonious work environment. Effective communication guarantees that employees are well-informed about company policies, goals, and expectations. It also encourages the free exchange of ideas, feedback, and concerns. Organizations can foster open communication by implementing regular meetings, surveys, suggestion boxes, and anonymous reporting channels. When employees feel heard as well as valued, they are more likely to be engaged and satisfied in their roles.

Fair treatment and equity are essential for creating a harmonious work environment. Employees should feel that they are treated fairly in matters related to hiring, compensation, promotions, and disciplinary actions. Organizations must have clear and equitable policies in place to ensure that decisions are based on merit rather than favoritism or bias. Fairness builds trust and confidence among employees, reducing the potential for resentment or conflicts arising from perceived injustices.

Effective conflict resolution mechanisms are crucial for maintaining harmony in the workplace. Conflicts are inevitable, but how they are addressed can significantly impact the work environment. Organizations should provide training in conflict resolution and establish processes for addressing disputes promptly and fairly. A well-designed conflict resolution framework encourages open communication, empathy, and constructive problem-solving, ensuring that conflicts do not fester and disrupt the workplace.

Promoting diversity and inclusion is necessary for creating a harmonious work environment. Organizations must actively seek diversity in their workforce and foster an inclusive culture that values differences. Inclusive practices ensure that all employees feel respected, valued, and included in decision-making processes. Diverse perspectives and backgrounds enrich the workplace and contribute to innovative solutions and creativity.

Employee well-being is a critical consideration in creating a harmonious work environment. Organizations should prioritize measures to support the physical and mental health of their employees. Encouraging employees with access to counseling services, flexible work schedules, and wellness programs can help them manage stress and to have a healthy work-life balance. Employee engagement, motivation, and satisfaction are all likely to increase when they perceive support for their well-being.

Recognition and appreciation are significant in fostering a harmonious work environment. Employees who feel valued and recognized for their contributions are more likely to be loyal and motivated. Organizations can implement recognition programs, celebrate milestones, and provide regular feedback to acknowledge and appreciate the efforts of their employees. Recognizing individual and team achievements helps build a positive work culture where employees feel encouraged and motivated to excel.

Leadership is pivotal in shaping the work environment. Efficient leaders set the tone for the organization and model the behaviors and values they expect from employees. Leaders should be approachable, empathetic, and responsive to employee needs and concerns. When leaders prioritize the well-being and development of their teams, they create an environment where trust and collaboration thrive.

Professional development opportunities are essential for creating a harmonious work environment. Companies should fund training and development initiatives that assist staff members in growing their careers and improving their skill sets. Employee engagement and commitment to their jobs are higher when they perceive opportunities for advancement within the company. Furthermore, offering coaching and mentoring programs can help employees grow and foster positive working relationships.

Initiatives promoting work-life balance are becoming more and more crucial for fostering a positive work environment. Employees should have the flexibility to manage their work schedules in a way that accommodates their personal lives and responsibilities. Remote work options, flexible hours, and generous leave policies can contribute to a healthier work-life balance. When employees can efficiently balance their work and personal lives, they are more likely to be content and productive.

Employee feedback and input should be actively sought and valued by organizations. Employees often have valuable insights and suggestions for improving processes and work conditions. Implementing feedback mechanisms and involving employees in decision-making processes can empower them to contribute to positive changes in the workplace. Engaging employees in shaping their work environment demonstrates that their opinions matter and that their well-being is a priority.

Ultimately, a harmonious work environment benefits both individuals and organizations in numerous ways. Employees in such an environment tend to be more engaged, motivated, as well as satisfied with their work. They are also more likely to collaborate effectively, leading to increased productivity and better results. Additionally, a harmonious work environment reduces turnover rates, as employees are more likely to stay with organizations that prioritize their well-being and professional growth.

In conclusion, creating and maintaining a harmonious work environment requires a multifaceted approach that involves fostering positive relationships, promoting open communication, ensuring fair treatment, and nurturing employee well-being. Organizations that prioritize these strategies not only enhance the satisfaction and productivity of their employees but also strengthen their overall performance and reputation. A harmonious work environment contributes to a culture of respect, trust, and collaboration, where individuals can thrive and organizations can excel.

CHAPTER X

Difficult Conversations in Personal Relationships

Dealing with family members

Family is a fundamental part of our lives, providing support, love, and a sense of belonging. However, family dynamics can also be complex, and at times, individuals may find themselves dealing with difficult family members. These difficulties can stem from an array of reasons, including personality clashes, differing values, or unresolved conflicts. Learning how to navigate these challenging relationships is essential for maintaining a sense of harmony within the family unit. In this section, we will explore strategies for dealing with difficult family members, including effective communication, setting boundaries, seeking understanding, and fostering forgiveness.

Effective communication is a foundational strategy for managing challenging family relationships. Clear and open communication helps in expressing feelings, concerns, and expectations while also allowing family members to understand each other better. When conflicts or misunderstandings arise, addressing them through calm and empathetic conversations can be a productive way to work through issues. It's important to actively listen to the perspectives of others and avoid reacting defensively, which can escalate tensions.

Setting boundaries is another crucial aspect of dealing with difficult family members. Boundaries define what behavior and treatment are acceptable or unacceptable within the family dynamic. Communicating these boundaries assertively and consistently is essential to ensure that family members understand and respect each other's limits. Setting boundaries can prevent family members from crossing lines that may lead to conflicts and resentment.

Seeking understanding and empathy can help uncover the underlying causes of difficult behavior within the family. Sometimes, difficult family members may be dealing with their own personal challenges or unresolved issues. Attempting to understand their perspective and emotions can foster empathy and pave the way for more compassionate interactions. Empathy can create an environment where family members feel heard and valued, making it easier to work through conflicts.

Fostering forgiveness is a powerful strategy for healing and improving relationships with difficult family members. Forgiveness does not mean condoning hurtful actions or behaviors but rather signifies a willingness to let go of resentment and anger. It allows individuals to move forward and rebuild trust within the family. Forgiveness can be a difficult procedure, but it can lead to emotional healing and the restoration of more harmonious relationships.

In some situations, seeking professional help may be necessary to address deeply ingrained conflicts or dynamics within the family. Family therapy or counseling can provide a safe and neutral space for family members to express their feelings, improve communication, and work through issues with the guidance of a trained therapist. Therapy can be especially beneficial when family conflicts are deeply rooted and resistant to resolution through individual efforts.

Practicing patience is essential when dealing with difficult family members. Resolving conflicts and fostering understanding may take time, and it's important to stay patient and persistent in your efforts. Recognize that change may not happen overnight and that family relationships are often complex and layered. Patience allows for gradual progress and healing.

Maintaining self-care is critical when dealing with difficult family members. The emotional toll of challenging family dynamics can be significant, leading to stress, anxiety, and even physical health issues. Engaging in self-care activities, such as mindfulness, exercise, and asking support from friends or a therapist, can help reduce the adverse effects of these interactions. Taking care of your well-being ensures that you have the emotional strength to address family challenges effectively.

Boundaries within the family are essential for managing difficult relationships. Setting boundaries means defining your limits and communicating them clearly to family members. For example, you can establish boundaries related to personal space, the topics of conversation, or the frequency of interactions. Boundaries help protect your emotional well-being and maintain a sense of control within the relationship.

Effective communication is a cornerstone of dealing with difficult family members. Open and honest communication can help address conflicts and misunderstandings. When discussing sensitive issues, it's important to use the "I" statements to express your feelings and avoid blaming or criticizing the other person. Active listening is similarly crucial, as it demonstrates your willingness to understand their perspective.

Conflict resolution skills are valuable when dealing with difficult family members. Conflicts within the family are inevitable, but how they are handled can significantly impact the outcome. Conflict resolution involves seeking mutually satisfactory solutions, rather than attempting to "win" the argument. Techniques such as compromise, negotiation, and finding common ground can be effective in resolving disputes and maintaining harmony within the family.

Understanding the perspective of difficult family members can provide insight into their behavior. Try to empathize with their emotions and experiences, even if you disagree with their actions. Consider whether there are underlying issues, past traumas, or unmet needs that may be contributing to their difficult behavior. Seeking understanding can help you approach the relationship with greater empathy and compassion.

Seeking professional guidance can be valuable when dealing with particularly challenging family dynamics. A trained therapist or counselor can facilitate family discussions, provide strategies for conflict resolution, and offer insights into improving communication. Family therapy can be especially effective in addressing deeply rooted issues and helping family members work through longstanding conflicts.

It's important to recognize that, in some cases, it may be necessary to limit or distance yourself from toxic or abusive family members. While it can be difficult to make such a decision, your emotional well-being and safety should always be a top priority. In extreme cases, seeking legal protection or restraining orders may be necessary.

In conclusion, dealing with difficult family members is a complex and emotionally challenging process. Effective communication, setting boundaries, seeking understanding, and fostering forgiveness are key strategies for managing these relationships. It's important to approach such situations with patience and self-care, recognizing that change may take time. In some situations, seeking professional help may be necessary to address deeply ingrained conflicts and dynamics within the family. Ultimately, the objective is to develop an environment where family members can work together to resolve conflicts, foster understanding, and build more harmonious relationships.

Handling conflicts in friendships and romantic relationships

Conflict is an inherent and inevitable part of any relationship, whether it's with a friend or a romantic partner. These conflicts can stem from differences in opinions, expectations, or even personality clashes. While conflicts in relationships are common, it's how they are managed and resolved that can determine the health and longevity of the relationship. Successful conflict resolution requires effective communication, empathy, compromise, and a commitment to maintaining the bond. In this section, we will explore strategies for handling conflicts in both friendships and romantic relationships, emphasizing the importance of communication, understanding, and the cultivation of emotional intelligence.

Effective communication is the cornerstone of addressing conflicts in friendships and romantic relationships. Transparent and honest communication allows individuals to express their thoughts, feelings, and concerns, fostering understanding and empathy. It is important to create a safe and non-judgmental space where both parties feel comfortable sharing their perspectives. When conflicts arise, initiating a calm and respectful conversation is essential. Using the "I" statements to express personal feelings and needs can help prevent defensive responses and encourage a more productive dialogue.

Listening actively and attentively is equally crucial during conflicts. Listening takes more than just hearing what is being said; it also involves observing the emotions and nonverbal cues of the speaker. Individuals are more likely to be open to finding common ground when they feel heard and understood. When the other person is speaking, refrain from interjecting, assuming anything, or drawing conclusions too quickly. Rather, give careful thought to understanding their perspective completely before answering.

One of the most effective tools for resolving disputes in relationships is empathy. Understanding and feeling another person's emotions is a necessary component of empathy. When conflicts arise, making an effort to see the situation from the other person's perspective can foster compassion and mutual understanding. Expressing empathy can de-escalate tension and create an atmosphere of cooperation rather than confrontation.

Compromise plays a crucial role in resolving conflicts in relationships. In any disagreement, it's unlikely that one party will get everything they want. Compromise involves finding middle ground and making concessions to meet the needs and desires of both individuals involved. It requires a willingness to prioritize the relationship over individual desires and ego. Compromise can lead to solutions that are mutually beneficial and strengthen the bond between friends or romantic partners.

Maintaining respect for one another, even during conflicts, is essential for the health of the relationship. Disagreements should not lead to disrespectful or hurtful behavior. Avoiding personal attacks, name-calling, or belittling remarks is crucial. Respecting boundaries as well as treating each other with kindness and courtesy even in the heat of an argument can help prevent conflicts from causing long-lasting damage to the relationship.

Time and space for reflection can be valuable when conflicts become overwhelming or emotional. Sometimes, taking a step back and allowing each person some space to cool off and collect their thoughts can lead to more productive discussions later on. It's important to communicate the need for a temporary break rather than simply withdrawing from the conversation, as this ensures that both individuals are on the same page.

Forgiveness is a critical aspect of resolving conflicts in relationships. Forgiveness involves letting go of past grievances and moving forward with the intention of healing and rebuilding the relationship. It is not about condoning hurtful actions but rather about choosing to release the anger and resentment that can poison a relationship. Forgiveness is a powerful tool for repairing trust and creating a path toward reconciliation.

In romantic relationships, maintaining emotional intimacy is key to conflict resolution. Emotional intimacy involves a deep connection that allows individuals to be vulnerable and share their thoughts and feelings honestly. Building emotional intimacy over time can create a foundation of trust and understanding that makes it easier to navigate conflicts. This connection allows individuals to express their emotions and concerns more openly and helps ensure that conflicts are addressed in a caring and supportive manner.

In friendships, loyalty and trust are essential for handling conflicts effectively. Trust involves believing in the reliability and integrity of the other person. When conflicts arise, it's important to remember the history and bond shared in the friendship. Trusting that the friend has good intentions and values the relationship can make it easier to work through disagreements.

In both friendships and romantic relationships, it's important to address conflicts promptly rather than letting them fester. Avoiding or suppressing conflicts can lead to resentment and the buildup of negative emotions. It's more productive to address issues as they arise, allowing both individuals to express their feelings and concerns and work toward resolution.

Seeking professional help or guidance from a counselor or therapist can be beneficial in handling particularly challenging conflicts in both friendships and romantic relationships. Therapists can provide a neutral and safe space for both individuals to express their concerns and work on solutions. Professional guidance can be especially helpful when conflicts are deeply rooted or persistent.

In conclusion, handling conflicts in friendships and romantic relationships requires effective communication, empathy, compromise, and a commitment to maintaining the bond. Conflicts are a natural part of any relationship, and the way they are managed can greatly impact the health and longevity of the connection. Open and honest communication, active listening, and the cultivation of empathy are essential skills for resolving conflicts. Additionally, prioritizing respect, forgiveness, and trust can help build stronger and more resilient relationships. Ultimately, successful conflict resolution in relationships is about preserving the connection and ensuring that both individuals continue to feel valued and supported.

Rebuilding trust after difficult conversations

Difficult conversations are an inevitable part of life, whether they occur in personal relationships, at work, or in various other contexts. These conversations often involve sensitive topics, differing viewpoints, or emotionally charged issues. While such conversations can be challenging, what follows them can be equally, if not more, crucial: the process of rebuilding trust. Healthy relationships depends on trust, and trust can be strained or destroyed following a difficult talk. In this section, we will explore the strategies and principles for rebuilding trust after difficult conversations, emphasizing the importance of effective communication, empathy, accountability, and consistency.

Effective communication is the linchpin of rebuilding trust after difficult conversations. It is essential to have an open and honest dialogue with the other party involved. Begin by recognizing the difficulty of the conversation and expressing your commitment to addressing the issues at hand. Emphasize your willingness to listen, understand, and work together toward a resolution. Creating a safe and non-judgmental space for continued communication is essential for rebuilding trust.

Listening actively and empathetically is a critical aspect of effective communication in the trust-building process. Actively listening involves giving the speaker your full attention, asking clarifying questions, and paraphrasing to ensure that you understand their perspective. It's important to acknowledge the emotions and concerns expressed by the other party. Empathy, or the ability to comprehend and share their feelings, helps convey that you genuinely care about their experience and are willing to validate their emotions.

Taking responsibility for your part in the difficult conversation is a crucial step in rebuilding trust. This includes acknowledging any mistakes, miscommunications, or misunderstandings that may have contributed to the conflict. Avoiding blame-shifting or defensiveness is essential. Instead, express genuine remorse if your actions or words caused harm and show a commitment to making amends and learning from the experience. Taking ownership of your role demonstrates accountability and can be a powerful step toward rebuilding trust.

Transparency and honesty are key principles in rebuilding trust. Be upfront and candid about your intentions, actions, and any relevant information. Hiding facts or withholding information can undermine trust and create further suspicion. Being transparent about your thoughts and feelings regarding the difficult conversation fosters an environment of openness and trustworthiness.

Consistency in your words and actions is essential in the trust-building process. Demonstrating reliability and predictability helps the other party feel secure and confident in the relationship. Be consistent in your efforts to address the issues discussed during the difficult conversation. Follow through on any commitments or agreements made, and ensure that your actions align with your words. Consistency builds a sense of dependability and reliability, which are vital components of trust.

Patience is a virtue when it comes to rebuilding trust after difficult conversations. Trust is not typically reestablished overnight, and the process may take time. Understand that the other party may need time to process their feelings and assess whether they can trust you again. Avoid rushing or pressuring them to forgive or rebuild trust hastily, as this can backfire and further damage the relationship.

Setting clear expectations for the future is an important step in the trust-building process. Discuss what both parties can do to prevent similar conflicts in the future and ensure that the relationship remains healthy. Establishing boundaries, communication guidelines, or conflict resolution strategies can help create a framework for building trust and preventing future difficulties.

In some cases, it may be beneficial to seek assistance from a neutral third party, like a mediator or a counselor, to facilitate the trust-building process. Mediators can help guide discussions, ensure that both parties are heard, and assist in finding common ground. Counselors can provide tools and techniques for rebuilding trust and offer support in addressing underlying issues that may have contributed to the difficult conversation.

Forgiveness is a pivotal aspect of rebuilding trust. Forgiveness entails letting go of anger, resentment, and negative emotions that may have resulted from the difficult conversation. It does not mean condoning harmful actions or forgetting about the conflict. Instead, forgiveness signifies a willingness to release the emotional burden and move forward with the hope of healing and rebuilding the relationship. Offering forgiveness can be a powerful gesture that demonstrates your commitment to the relationship's well-being.

Rebuilding trust after difficult conversations often requires a commitment to personal growth and self-improvement. Reflect on your own behaviors and communication styles, and consider how they may have contributed to the conflict. Seek opportunities for self-awareness and self-improvement, such as personal development workshops, therapy, or communication skills training. Demonstrating your dedication to personal growth can help rebuild trust by showing that you are actively working to become a better partner in the relationship.

In conclusion, rebuilding trust after difficult conversations is a complex and sensitive process that requires effective communication, empathy, accountability, and consistency. Trust is a fragile and valuable asset in any relationship, and when it is damaged, the road to recovery can be challenging. However, with patience, openness, and a genuine commitment to rebuilding trust, it is possible to heal and strengthen relationships that have been tested by difficult conversations. The principles outlined in this section serve as a roadmap for those seeking to rebuild trust and nurture healthier and more resilient relationships.

CHAPTER XI

Strategies for Long-Term Improvement

Continuing to develop communication skills

An essential element of human interaction that permeates every facet of our lives is communication. Effective communication is crucial not only for personal relationships but also for professional success and social interactions. It involves the exchange of ideas, emotions, information, and understanding. While we all possess some level of communication skills, the process of developing and improving these skills should be a lifelong journey. In this section, we will explore the importance of continuing to develop communication skills, strategies for enhancing them, and the benefits of proficient communication in various aspects of life.

Effective communication skills are crucial for developing and maintaining healthy relationships. Whether in personal relationships, friendships, or romantic partnerships, clear and open communication is the foundation of trust, understanding, and emotional intimacy. The capacity to express thoughts and feelings honestly and respectfully is key to resolving conflicts, navigating challenges, and fostering mutual respect and connection. Continually developing communication skills in relationships allows individuals to convey love, empathy, and support, ultimately contributing to more fulfilling and harmonious connections.

In the workplace, strong communication skills are paramount for professional growth and success. Employers value employees that can articulate their ideas, collaborate effectively with colleagues, and convey information clearly and persuasively. Proficient communication skills also extend to active listening, empathy, and the ability to offer constructive feedback. Continued development of communication skills can enhance one's performance, aid in career advancement, and foster positive workplace relationships.

The benefits of improving communication skills are not limited to personal and professional domains; they extend to broader social interactions. Effective communication is the bridge that links people from diverse backgrounds, cultures, and perspectives. Developing communication skills that are sensitive to cultural differences, nuances, and non-verbal cues can lead to more inclusive and respectful interactions in a multicultural world. It promotes understanding, reduces misunderstandings, and encourages empathy and cooperation.

One essential aspect of developing communication skills is active listening. Active listening involves giving the speaker full attention, refraining from interrupting, and demonstrating genuine interest in what they are saying. It also includes non-verbal cues, such as maintaining eye contact, nodding, and providing verbal feedback to indicate that you are engaged in the conversation. Active listening not only enhances understanding but also fosters empathy and respect for the speaker's perspective. Practicing active listening consistently can significantly improve one's overall communication skills.

Another essential element of effective communication is empathy. Empathy entails understanding and sharing the emotions and perspectives of others. It is the ability to place oneself in someone else's shoes and appreciate their feelings and experiences. Cultivating empathy allows individuals to connect on a deeper level with others, fostering stronger bonds and more meaningful relationships. Empathetic communication involves validating the emotions of the other person and conveying understanding and support.

Conflict resolution is an area where effective communication skills are particularly valuable. Conflicts are an inevitable part of human interactions, and how they are handled can greatly impact the outcome. Effective conflict resolution involves active listening, empathy, and assertive communication. It requires individuals to express their concerns and feelings honestly while also being open to understanding the perspective of the other party. Practicing constructive conflict resolution techniques, such as negotiation, compromise, and problem-solving, can lead to mutually satisfactory solutions and strengthen relationships.

Continuing to develop communication skills also means refining one's ability to adapt to different communication styles and preferences. People have varying communication preferences, including verbal, written, visual, or kinesthetic forms of communication. Recognizing and adapting to these preferences allows individuals to communicate more effectively with an array of people. For example, in a professional setting, one may need to adapt their communication style when interacting with a manager, colleague, or client to ensure that the message is well-received.

The digital age has introduced new forms of communication, including email, social media, and video conferencing. Developing digital communication skills is increasingly important in today's interconnected world. This includes mastering the art of writing clear and concise emails, effectively conveying ideas through digital platforms, and understanding the nuances of virtual communication. Effective digital communication is critical for professional success and maintaining relationships in the digital era.

Public speaking and presentation skills are necessary for those in leadership roles, but they are valuable for anyone seeking to improve their communication abilities. Public speaking involves conveying ideas, information, or messages to an audience. It requires not only clear and organized content but also effective delivery, including voice modulation, body language, and engagement with the audience. Developing public speaking skills can boost confidence, influence others, and improve one's ability to convey messages persuasively.

Technology offers a wealth of resources for individuals seeking to continue developing their communication skills. Online courses, webinars, and workshops cover a wide range of communication topics, from public speaking and conflict resolution to active listening and empathy. These resources provide the opportunity to learn and practice communication skills in a structured and interactive environment. Additionally, many organizations offer communication training as part of their professional development programs.

Peer feedback and self-assessment are valuable tools for improving communication skills. Seeking feedback from colleagues, friends, or mentors can provide insights into areas that may need improvement. Self-assessment involves reflecting on one's communication experiences and identifying areas for growth. Regularly evaluating one's communication skills and seeking feedback from others can accelerate the development process.

In conclusion, the importance of continuing to develop communication skills cannot be overstated. Effective communication is the linchpin of healthy relationships, professional success, and harmonious social interactions. It involves active listening, empathy, conflict resolution, and the ability to adapt to diverse communication styles.

Developing communication skills is an ongoing journey that requires self-awareness, practice, and a commitment to growth. The benefits of proficient communication extend to all areas of life, enriching personal relationships, enhancing professional opportunities, and fostering understanding in a diverse and interconnected world.

Maintaining healthy relationships

Healthy relationships are crucial to living a happy and purposeful life. The quality of our relationships—whether they be with friends, family, romantic partners, or coworkers—has a significant impact on our general wellbeing. Healthy relationships bring joy, support, and a sense of belonging, while unhealthy ones can cause stress, anxiety, and unhappiness. Maintaining healthy relationships is a lifelong endeavor that requires effort, communication, empathy, and a commitment to mutual growth and respect. In this section, we will explore the importance of maintaining healthy relationships, the key principles that underlie them, and strategies for nurturing and sustaining these valuable connections.

Healthy relationships are vital for emotional well-being and mental health. They provide a source of comfort, security, and emotional support during life's ups and downs. Knowing that we have people we can rely on and confide in fosters resilience and enhances our ability to cope with stress as well as adversity. Healthy relationships offer a safe space for expressing emotions, seeking advice, and finding solace, contributing significantly to our overall happiness and mental well-being.

Trust is the bedrock of every healthy relationships. Trust is built on reliability, honesty, and consistency in words and actions. Trust means having confidence in the other person's intentions and knowing that they have your best interests at heart. Trust is not given lightly; it is earned over time through consistent behavior and open communication. Maintaining trust requires transparency, accountability, and a commitment to keeping one's promises.

Effective communication is another fundamental aspect of maintaining healthy relationships. Communication involves not only expressing feelings, thoughts, and demands but also actively listening to and understanding the perspectives of others. Healthy communication is characterized by honesty, respect, and empathy. It is the key to resolving conflicts, preventing misunderstandings, and building a deeper connection. Maintaining open lines of communication guarantees that both parties feel heard, valued, and understood.

Empathy is the capacity to comprehend as well as share the feelings and perspectives of others. It is a cornerstone of healthy relationships because it fosters compassion, validation, and a deeper emotional connection. Empathy means putting oneself in the other person's shoes and appreciating their experiences and emotions. Practicing empathy allows individuals to provide emotional support, validate each other's feelings, and demonstrate care and understanding.

Respect is a core principle in maintaining healthy relationships. Respect means valuing the other person's autonomy, boundaries, and individuality. It entails treating each other with kindness, courtesy, and consideration. In healthy relationships, respect extends to differences in opinions, beliefs, and choices. Respecting each other's autonomy means allowing space for individual growth and decision-making while still nurturing the bond.

Conflict is a natural part of any relationship, but how conflicts are handled can significantly impact their outcome. Healthy relationships require effective conflict resolution skills. Conflict resolution involves addressing disagreements and misunderstandings in a constructive and respectful manner. It means expressing concerns and feelings honestly, listening actively to the other person's perspective, and working together to find mutually satisfactory solutions. Healthy conflict resolution techniques promote understanding, compromise, and growth.

Boundaries are essential for maintaining healthy relationships. Boundaries define what behavior and treatment are acceptable or unacceptable within the relationship. Clear and respectful communication of boundaries ensures that both parties understand as well as respect each other's limits. Boundaries protect individual autonomy and emotional well-being while also contributing to a sense of safety and comfort within the relationship.

Forgiveness is a pivotal aspect of maintaining healthy relationships. Forgiveness involves letting go of past grievances and moving forward with the intention of healing and rebuilding the relationship. It signifies a willingness to release anger, resentment, and negative emotions. Forgiveness does not mean condoning harmful actions or forgetting about conflicts; rather, it offers the opportunity for emotional healing and the restoration of trust and connection.

Time and attention are necessary investments in maintaining healthy relationships. Spending quality time together allows individuals to strengthen their bonds, create cherished memories, and nurture their connection. In today's fast-paced world, making time for loved ones can be challenging, but prioritizing the relationship demonstrates its significance and value.

Support and encouragement are hallmarks of healthy relationships. Supporting each other's goals, dreams, and aspirations promotes a sense of partnership and mutual growth. Encouraging each other to pursue personal interests and ambitions enhances individual well-being and enriches the relationship. Providing emotional support during difficult times, celebrating successes, and offering words of encouragement are gestures that strengthen the bond.

Fostering a sense of equality and balance in the relationship is crucial for its sustainability. Healthy relationships are built on the premise of shared responsibilities, decision-making, and contributions. Both parties should feel that their needs, opinions, and contributions are valued and respected. Imbalances in power or decision-making can lead to resentment and strain the relationship.

Shared values and goals are important for maintaining healthy relationships. While differences can be enriching, having common values and goals can create a sense of unity and purpose. Shared values provide a foundation for decision-making and problem-solving, while shared goals give the relationship direction and motivation.

Adaptability and flexibility are important qualities for navigating the challenges that life inevitably brings to relationships. Circumstances change, and individuals evolve. Healthy relationships require the capacity to adapt to these changes and grow together. Being open to compromise, adjusting expectations, and accommodating each other's needs contribute to the relationship's resilience and longevity.

Regular check-ins and discussions about the state of the relationship can be beneficial for maintaining its health. These conversations provide an opportunity to assess the relationship's strengths and areas for improvement. It permits both parties to express their feelings, needs, and concerns openly. Regular check-ins demonstrate a commitment to the relationship's growth and well-being.

In conclusion, maintaining healthy relationships is a lifelong endeavor that requires effort, communication, empathy, and a commitment to mutual growth and respect. Healthy relationships contribute significantly to our emotional well-being and mental health, providing a source of comfort, support, and happiness. Trust, effective communication, empathy, respect, and conflict resolution are the foundational principles of healthy relationships. Investing time, attention, and effort into relationships, while also fostering a sense of equality, shared values, and adaptability, ensures their sustainability and long-term fulfillment. Ultimately, healthy relationships enrich our lives and provide a sense of connection and belonging that is invaluable.

Self-care and self-reflection

In today's fast-paced and demanding world, it is easy to become overwhelmed by the daily stresses and responsibilities of life. Amid these challenges, we often neglect the most important aspect of our well-being: ourselves. Self-care and self-reflection are two interconnected practices that are pivotal in maintaining our physical, emotional, and mental health. They provide us with the tools to nurture our inner selves, find balance, and lead more fulfilling lives. In this section, we will explore the significance of self-care and self-reflection, their individual components, and how they intertwine to foster personal growth, resilience, and a deeper understanding of ourselves.

Self-care is a holistic approach to nourishing our well-being. It encompasses an array of activities and practices that prioritize self-preservation, restoration, and self-compassion. Physical self-care implicates taking care of our bodies through exercise, a balanced diet, adequate sleep, and regular medical check-ups. Emotional self-care focuses on managing and expressing our feelings constructively, seeking support when needed, and practicing self-compassion and self-acceptance. Mental self-care involves participating in activities that stimulate the mind, such as reading, learning, or creative pursuits, while also managing stress and practicing mindfulness. Social self-care emphasizes nurturing healthy relationships, setting boundaries, and fostering connections with others. Spiritual self-care centers around exploring our values, beliefs, and purpose in life, often through practices like meditation, prayer, or spending time in nature.

The importance of self-care cannot be overstated, as it directly affects our physical as well as mental health. Neglecting self-care can result in burnout, chronic stress, and a host of physical and emotional health issues. By prioritizing self-care, we not only enhance our overall well-being but also improve our capacity to navigate life's challenges effectively. Self-care serves as a foundation for personal growth and resilience, allowing us to cope with stress, bounce back from setbacks, and keep a balanced and fulfilling life.

Self-reflection is the practice of assessing our thoughts, feelings, and experiences in a thoughtful and contemplative manner. It involves taking a step back from the busyness of life to gain insight into our values, beliefs, goals, and behaviors. Self-reflection is a journey of self-discovery that allows us to understand ourselves more deeply, make informed choices, and grow as individuals. It can take various forms, including journaling, meditation, mindfulness, therapy, or simply setting aside time for introspection.

Self-reflection helps us gain clarity about our goals and values, enabling us to align our actions with our authentic selves. It permits us to recognize patterns of behavior and thought that may be holding us back or causing unnecessary stress. By examining our experiences and reactions, we can identify areas for personal growth and self-improvement. Self-reflection also facilitates emotional intelligence, as it helps us understand our own emotions and empathize with the feelings and perspectives of others.

The connection between self-care and self-reflection is profound. Self-reflection is a form of self-care in itself, as it encourages us to prioritize our mental and emotional well-being. Engaging in self-reflection is an act of self-compassion, allowing us to acknowledge our thoughts and feelings without judgment. It provides a safe space for exploring our inner world, gaining perspective, and finding solutions to life's challenges. Self-reflection can lead to greater self-awareness, which is the foundation of effective self-care.

Self-care and self-reflection work together to create a cycle of personal growth and well-being. Self-care practices, such as mindfulness meditation, can enhance self-reflection by quieting the mind and facilitating introspection. Conversely, self-reflection can lead to more intentional and effective self-care practices. For example, through self-reflection, we may recognize that we need to set boundaries in our relationships to reduce stress, leading to a self-care practice of assertiveness. The synergy between these two practices fosters resilience and helps us navigate life's challenges with greater ease.

One of the benefits of self-reflection is the development of a growth mindset. A growth mindset is known as the belief that we can grow, learn, and improve throughout our lives. It is the opposite of a fixed mindset, which assumes that our capacities and intelligence are static. Engaging in self-reflection encourages us to view our experiences, successes, and failures as opportunities for growth and learning. This mindset shift can significantly impact our self-care practices, as we become more open to trying new self-care activities, seeking support, and adapting to changing circumstances.

Another valuable aspect of self-reflection is its role in stress management. By examining our thoughts and reactions in a mindful and non-judgmental way, we can identify sources of stress and establish strategies for coping with them effectively. Self-reflection can help us recognize negative thought patterns and change them with more constructive and positive ones. This can lead to significant emotional resilience and a reduction in stress-related health issues.

Self-care and self-reflection also contribute to our overall resilience in the face of adversity. Resilience is the ability to bounce back from challenges and setbacks. When we engage in regular self-care practices and self-reflection, we develop a strong foundation of well-being that can serve as a buffer during difficult times. These practices enhance our emotional intelligence, allowing us to navigate complex emotions and relationships with greater skill and empathy. This emotional resilience is a valuable asset in personal and professional life, as it helps us weather storms, adapt to change, and maintain a positive outlook even in challenging circumstances.

Incorporating self-care and self-reflection into our daily lives requires intention and commitment. It is a journey of self-discovery and personal growth that evolves over time. To start, it can be helpful to set aside dedicated time for self-care and self-reflection in your routine. This can be as simple as allocating a few minutes each day for mindfulness meditation or journaling. It is essential to approach self-care and self-reflection with an open and non-judgmental attitude, as these practices are about self-compassion and self-acceptance.

Seeking support and guidance from a counselor, therapist, or coach can also be beneficial in incorporating self-care and self-reflection into your life. These professionals can provide tools, techniques, and insights tailored to your specific needs and goals. They can help you navigate challenges, gain clarity about your values and priorities, and develop a personalized self-care and self-reflection plan.

In conclusion, self-care and self-reflection are powerful practices that contribute to our emotional, physical, as well as mental well-being. They are interconnected, with self-reflection enhancing our self-care practices and vice versa. Self-care involves nurturing various aspects of our lives, including physical, emotional, mental, social, and spiritual well-being. Self-reflection, on the other hand, is the practice of examining our thoughts, feelings, and experiences with curiosity and compassion. Together, these practices foster personal growth, resilience, and a deeper understanding of ourselves. Incorporating self-care and self-reflection into our daily lives is an ongoing journey of self-discovery as well as self-improvement, ultimately leading to a more balanced, fulfilling, and meaningful life.

CONCLUSION

In "The Challenging Conversation: Skills and Strategies for Dealing with Difficult People," we have embarked on a journey through the intricate landscape of human interactions. Throughout this book, we have explored a multitude of valuable tools and insights that equip us to navigate the complexities of challenging conversations with confidence and grace.

From understanding the diverse types of difficult personalities to delving deep into the psychological insights behind their behavior, we have gained a profound awareness of the intricacies at play. We have learned that difficult people come in various forms, each with their unique triggers and motivations, and that empathy and understanding can be powerful allies in bridging the gap between us and them.

We have honed our skills in setting clear boundaries, practicing assertiveness, and employing the "EAR" approach—Empathize, Assert, Redirect—to create a harmonious and constructive dialogue. We have harnessed the power of active listening, non-verbal communication cues, and effective questioning to foster understanding and connection, even in the most challenging of circumstances.

As we conclude this journey, we recognize that the art of dealing with difficult people is not merely a set of techniques but a profound transformation of our approach to human interaction. It is about fostering empathy, building bridges, and finding common ground. It is about nurturing healthier relationships and protecting our well-being.

In the end, "The Challenging Conversation" reminds us that every interaction is a possibility for growth and connection, and that with the right skills and strategies, we can transform challenging conversations into transformative experiences. So, as you embark on your own journey of communication and connection, may this book serve as a guide and companion, empowering you to navigate the intricacies of human relationships with wisdom, resilience, and empathy.

Thank you for buying and reading/ listening to our book. If you found this book useful/ helpful please take a few minutes and leave a review on the platform where you purchased our book. Your feedback matters greatly to us.